Ednah D. Harmon Wickson

Sag Harbor
1906.

# THE GENTLE READER

# The Gentle Reader

BY

## SAMUEL McCHORD CROTHERS

BOSTON AND NEW YORK

HOUGHTON, MIFFLIN AND COMPANY

The Riverside Press, Cambridge

# Preface

WHEN Don Quixote was descanting on the beauty of the peerless Dulcinea, the Duchess interrupted him by expressing a doubt as to that lady's existence.

"Much may be said on that point," said Don Quixote. "God only knows whether there be any Dulcinea or not in the world. These are things the proof of which must not be pushed to extreme lengths."

But this admission does not in the least interfere with the habitual current of his thoughts, or cool the ardor of his loyalty. He proceeds after the momentary digression as if nothing had happened. "I behold her as she needs must be, a lady who contains within herself all the qualities to make her famous throughout the world; beautiful, without blemish; dignified, without haughtiness; tender, and yet modest; gracious from courtesy, and courteous from good breeding; and lastly of illustrious birth."

If in the following pages I begin by admitting that there is much to be said in behalf of the popular notion that the Gentle Reader no longer exists, let this pass simply as an evidence of my decent respect for the opinion of mankind. To my mind the Gentle Reader is the most agreeable of companions, and to make his acquaintance is one of the pleasures of life.

Of so elusive a personality it is not always possible to give a consistent account. I have no doubt that I may have occasionally attributed to him sentiments which are really my own; on the other hand, I suspect that some views that I have set down as my own may have been unconsciously derived from him. I have particular reference to the opinions expressed on the

subject of Ignorance.. Such confusion of mental
properties the Gentle Reader will readily pardon, for there is no one in all the world so
careless of the distinctions between Meum and
Tuum.

# CONTENTS

# The Gentle Reader

---

WHAT has become of the Gentle Reader?
One does not like to think that he has
passed away with the stagecoach and the weekly
news-letter; and that henceforth we are to be
confronted only by the stony glare of the Intelligent Reading Public. Once upon a time, that
is to say a generation or two ago, he was very
highly esteemed. To him books were dedicated,
with long rambling prefaces and with episodes
which were their own excuse for being. In the
very middle of the story the writer would stop
with a word of apology or explanation addressed
to the Gentle Reader, or at the very least with a
nod or a wink. No matter if the fate of the hero
be in suspense or the plot be inextricably involved.

"Hang the plot!" says the author. "I must

have a chat with the Gentle Reader, and find out what he thinks about it."

And so confidences were interchanged, and there was gossip about the Universe and suggestions in regard to the queerness of human nature, until, at last, the author would jump up with, "Enough of this, Gentle Reader; perhaps it's time to go back to the story."

The thirteenth book of Tom Jones leaves the heroine in the greatest distress. The last words are, "Nor did this thought once suffer her to close her eyes during the whole succeeding night." Had Fielding been addressing the Intelligent Modern Public he would have intensified the interest by giving an analysis of Sophia's distress so that we should all share her insomnia. But not at all! While the dear girl is recovering her spirits it is such an excellent opportunity to have uninterrupted discourse with the Gentle Reader, who doesn't take these things too hard, having long since come to "the years that bring the philosophic mind." So the next chapter is entitled An Essay to prove that an author will write better for having some knowledge of the subject on which he treats. The discussion is altogether irrelevant; that is what the Gentle Reader likes.

"It is a paradoxical statement you make," he says, trying to draw the author out. "What are your arguments?"

Then the author moderates his expressions. "To say the truth I require no more than that an author should have some little knowledge of the subject of which he treats."

"That sounds more reasonable," says the Gentle Reader. "You know how much I dislike extreme views. Let us admit, for the sake of argument, that a writer may know a little about his subject. I hope that this may not prove the opening wedge for erudition. By the way, where was it we left the sweet Sophy; and do you happen to know anything more about that scapegrace Jones?"

That was the way books were written and read in the good old days before the invention of the telephone and the short story. The generation that delighted in Fielding and Richardson had some staying power. A book was something to tie to. No one would say jauntily, "I have read Sir Charles Grandison," but only, "I am reading." The characters of fiction were not treated as transient guests, but as lifelong companions destined to be a solace in old age. The short story, on the other hand, is invented for people who want a literary " quick lunch." "Tell me a story while I wait," demands the eager devourer of fiction. "Serve it hot, and be mighty quick about it!"

In rushes the story-teller with love, marriage, jealousy, disillusion, and suicide all served up together before you can say Jack Robinson. There is no time for explanation, and the reader is in no mood to allow it. As for the suicide, it must end that way; for it is the quickest. The ending, "They were happy ever after," cannot be allowed, for the doting author can never resist the temptation to add another chapter, dated ten years after, to show how happy they were.

I sometimes fear that reading, in the old-fashioned sense, may become a lost art. The habit of resorting to the printed page for information is an excellent one, but it is not what I have in mind. A person wants something and knows where to get it. He goes to a book just as he goes to a department store. Knowledge is a commodity done up in a neat parcel. So that the article is well made he does not care either for the manufacturer or the dealer.

Literature, properly so called, is quite different from this, and literary values inhere not in things or even in ideas, but in persons. There are some rare spirits that have imparted themselves to their words. The book then becomes a person, and reading comes to be a kind of conversation. The reader is not passive, as if he were listening to a lecture on The Ethics of the Babylonians. He is sitting by his fireside, and old friends drop in on him. He knows their habits and whims, and is glad to see them and to interchange thought. They are perfectly at their ease, and there is all the time in the world, and if he yawns now and then nobody is offended, and if he prefers to follow a thought of his own rather than theirs there is no discourtesy in leaving them. If his friends are dull this evening, it is because he would have it so ; that is why he invited them. He wants to have a good, cosy, dull time. He has had enough to stir him up during the day ; now he wants to be let down. He knows a score of good old au-

thors who have lived long in the happy poppy
fields.

In all good faith he invokes the goddess of the
Dunciad : —

> " Her ample presence fills up all the place,
> A veil of fogs dilates her awful face.
> Here to her Chosen all her works she shews,
> Prose swelled to verse, verse loitering into prose."

The Gentle Reader nods placidly and joins in
the ascription : —

> " Great tamer of all human art!
> First in my care and ever at my heart;
> Dullness whose good old cause I still defend.
> . . . . . . . . .
> O ever gracious to perplex'd mankind,
> Still shed a healing mist before the mind;
> And lest we err by wit's wild dancing light,
> Secure us kindly in our native night."

I would not call any one a gentle reader who
does not now and then take up a dull book, and
enjoy it in the spirit in which it was written.

Wise old Burton, in the Anatomy of Melancholy, advises the restless person to " read some
pleasant author till he be asleep." Many persons
find the Anatomy of Melancholy to answer this
purpose; though Dr. Johnson declares that it

was the only book that took him out of bed two
hours before he wished to rise. It is hard to
draw the line between stimulants and narcotics.

This insistence on the test of the enjoyment
of the dullness of a dull book is not arbitrary.
It arises from the characteristic of the Gentle
Reader. He takes a book for what it is and
never for what it is not. If he does n't like it at
all he does n't read it. If he does read it, it is
because he likes its real quality. That is the
way we do with our friends. They are the people of whom we say that "we get at them." I
suppose every one of us has some friend of whom
we would confess that as thinker he is inferior to
Plato. But we like him no less for that. We
might criticise him if we cared, — but we never
care. We prefer to take him as he is. It is the
flavor of his individuality that we enjoy. Appreciation of literature is the getting at an author,
so that we like what he is, while all that he is not
is irrelevant.

There are those who endeavor to reduce literary
criticism to an exact science. To this end they
would eliminate the personal element, and subject our admirations to fixed standards. In this

way it is hoped that we may ultimately be able
to measure the road to Parnassus by kilometers.
All this is much more easily said than done.
Personal likings will not stay eliminated. We
admire the acuteness of the critic who reveals the
unsuspected excellence of our favorite writer. It
is a pleasure like that which comes when a friend
is received into a learned society. We don't
know much about his learning, but we know that
he is a good fellow, and we are glad to learn that
he is getting on. We feel also a personal satisfaction in having our tastes vindicated and our
enjoyment treated as if it were a virtue, just as
Mr. Pecksniff was pleased with the reflection that
while he was eating his dinner, he was at the
same time obeying a law of the Universe.

But the rub comes when the judgment of the
critic disagrees with ours. We discover that his
laws have no penalties, and that if we get more
enjoyment from breaking than from obeying,
then we are just that much ahead. As for giving
up an author just because the judgment of the
critic is against him, who ever heard of such a
thing? The stanchest canons of criticism are
exploded by a genuine burst of admiration.

That is what happens whenever a writer of original force appears. The old rules do not explain him, so we must make new rules. We first enjoy him, and then we welcome the clever persons who assure us that the enjoyment is greatly to our credit. But —

> "You must love him ere to you
> He shall seem worthy of your love."

I asked a little four-year-old critic, whose literary judgments I accept as final, what stories she liked best. She answered, "I like Joseph and Aladdin and The Forty Thieves and The Probable Son."

It was a purely individual judgment. Some day she may learn that she has the opinion of many centuries behind her. When she studies rhetoric she may be able to tell why Aladdin is better than The Shaving of Shagpat, and why the story of "The Probable Son" delights her, while the half-hour homily on the parable makes not the slightest impression on her mind. The fact is, she knows a good story just as she knows a good apple. How the flavor got there is a scientific question which she has not considered;

but being there, trust the uncloyed palate to find it out! She does not set up as a superior person having good taste; but she says, " I can tell you what tastes good."

The Gentle Reader is not greatly drawn to any formal treatises. He does not enjoy a bare bit of philosophy that has been moulded into a fixed form. Yet he dearly loves a philosopher, especially if he turns out to be a sensible sort of man who does n't put on airs.

He likes the old Greek way of philosophizing. What a delight it was for him to learn that the Academy in Athens was not a white building with green blinds set upon a bleak hilltop, but a grove where, on pleasant days, Plato could be found, ready to talk with all comers! That was something like; no board of trustees, no written examinations, no text-books — just Plato! You never knew what was to be the subject or where you were coming out; all you were sure of was that you would come away with a new idea. Or if you tired of the Academy, there were the Peripatetics, gentlemen who were drawn together because they imagined they could think better on their legs; or there were the Stoics, elderly per-

sons who liked to sit on the porch and discuss
the "cosmic weather." No wonder the Greeks
got such a reputation as philosophers! They
deserve no credit for it. Any one would like
philosophy were it served up in that way.

All that has passed. Were Socrates to come
back and enter a downtown office to inquire after
the difference between the Good and the Beautiful, he would be confronted with one of those
neatly printed cards, intended to discourage the
Socratic method during business hours: "This
is our busy day."

The Gentle Reader also has his business hours,
and has learned to submit to their inexorable requirements; but now and then he has a few
hours to himself. He declines an invitation to a
progressive euchre party, on the ground of a previous engagement he had made long ago, in his
college days, to meet some gentlemen of the fifth
century B. C. The evening passes so pleasantly,
and the world seems so much fresher in interest,
that he wonders why he does n't do that sort of
thing oftener. Perhaps there are some other
progressive euchre parties he could cut, and the
world be none the worse.

How many people there have been who have gone through the world with their eyes open, and who have jotted down their impressions by the way! How quickly these philosophers come to know their own. Listen to Izaak Walton in his Epistle to the Reader: "I think it fit to tell thee these following truths, that I did not undertake to write or publish this discourse of Fish and Fishing to please myself, and that I wish it may not displease others. And yet I cannot doubt but that by it some readers may receive so much profit that if they be not very busy men, may make it not unworthy the time of their perusal. And I wish the reader to take notice that in the writing of it I have made a recreation of a re- creation; and that it might prove so to thee in the reading, and not to read dully and tediously, I have in several places mixed some innocent mirth; of which if thou be a severe, sour-com- plexioned man, then I here disallow thee to be a competent judge. . . . I am the willinger to jus- tify this innocent mirth because the whole dis- course is a kind of picture of my own disposition, at least of my disposition on such days and times as I allow myself — when Nat and I go fishing

together." How cleverly he bows out the ichthy-
ologists! How he rebukes the sordid creature
who has come simply to find out how to catch
fish! That is the very spirit of Simon Magus!
" Thou hast neither part nor lot in this matter!"

The Gentle Reader has no ulterior aims. All
he wants to know is how Izaak Walton felt when
he went fishing, and what he was thinking about.

"A kind of picture of a man's own disposition," that is literature. Even the most futile
attempt at self-revelation evokes sympathy. I
remember, as a boy, gazing at an austere volume
in my grandfather's library. It was, as far as I
could ascertain, an indigestible mixture of theology and philology. But my eye was caught by
the title, The Diversions of Purley. I had not
the slightest idea who Purley was, but my heart
went out to him at once.

" Poor Purley!" I said. "If these were your
diversions, what a dog's life you must have led!"
I could see Purley gazing vaguely through his
spectacles as he said: " Don't pity me! It's
true I have had my trials, — but then again what
larks! See that big book; I did it!" Only
long after did I learn that my sympathy was un-

called for, as Purley was not a person but a place.

Of all the devices for promoting a good understanding the old-fashioned Preface was the most excellent. It was not an introduction to the subject, its purpose was personal. In these days the Preface, where it survives, is reduced to the smallest possible space. It is like the platform of an electric car which affords the passenger a precarious foothold while he strives to obey the stern demand of the conductor that he move forward. But time was when the Preface was the broad hospitable porch on which the Author and Reader sat for an hour or so and talked over the enterprise that was before them. Sometimes they would talk so long that they almost forgot their ostensible subject.

The very title of Sir William Davenant's "Preface before Gondibert" suggests the hospitable leisure of the seventeenth century. Gondibert is a poetical masterpiece not to be lightly adventured upon. The mind must be duly prepared for it. Sir William, therefore, discourses about poetry in general, and then takes up special instances.

"I will (according as all times have applied their reverence) begin with Homer."

"Homer is an admirable point of departure, and I have no doubt but that you will also tell what you think of Virgil," says the Gentle Reader, who when he is asked to go a mile is glad to go twain.

Then follows discourse on Lucan, Statius, Tasso, and the rest.

"But I feel (sir) that I am falling into the dangerous Fit of a hot writer; for instead of performing the promise which begins this Preface, and doth oblige me (after I had given you the judgement of some upon others), to present myself to your censure, I am wandering after new thoughts; but I shall ask your pardon and return to my undertaking."

"No apologies are necessary, I assure you. With new thoughts the rule is first come, first served, while an immortal masterpiece can wait till such time as we can enjoy it together."

After some reflections on the fallibility of the clergy and the state of the country, the author proceeds to describe the general structure of his poem.

"I have now given you an account of such provisions as I have made for this new Building, and you may next please, having examined the substance, to take a view of the form." He points out the "shadowings, happy strokes, and sweet graces" of his work. This is done with an intimacy of knowledge and fullness of appreciation that could not be possible in a stranger.

"'T is now fit, after I have given you so long a survey of the Building, to render you some account of the Builder, that you may know by what times, pains, and assistance I have already proceeded."

The time passes with much pleasure and profit until at last the host says: "And now (sir) I shall after my busy vanitie in shewing and describing my new Building, with great quietness, being almost as weary as yourself, bring you to the Back-dore."

It is all so handsomely done that the reader is prepared to begin upon the poem itself, and would do so were it not that the distinguished friend of the author, Mr. Hobbes, has prepared An Answer to the Preface — a point of politeness which has not survived the seventeenth century. Mr. Hobbes is of the opinion that there is only one point in which Gondibert is inferior to the masterpieces of antiquity, and that is that it is written in English instead of in Greek or Latin. The Preface and Answer to the Preface having been read, the further discovery is made that there is a Postscript.

The Author, it appears, has fallen on evil days, and is in prison charged with High Treason.

"I am arrived here at the middle of the Third Book which makes an equal half of the Poem, and I was now by degrees to present you (as I promised in the Preface) the several keys to the Main Building, which should convey you through such short walks as give you an easie view of the whole Frame. But 't is high time to strike sail and cast anchor (though I have but run half my course), when at the Helme I am threatened with Death, who though he can trouble us but once seems troublesome, and even in the Innocent may beget such gravitie as diverts the Musick of Verse. I beseech thee if thou art as civill as to be pleased with what is written, not to take it ill that I run not till my last gasp. . . . If thou art a malicious Reader thou wilt remember my Pre-

face boldly confessed that a main motive to this
undertaking was a desire of Fame, and thou maist
likewise say that I may not possibly live to enjoy it.
. . . If thou (Reader) art one of those who has
been warmed with Poetick Fire, I reverence thee
as my Judge, and whilst others tax me with Vanitie as if the Preface argued my good Opinion
of the Work, I appeal to thy Conscience whether
it be much more than such a necessary assurance
as thou hast made to thyself in like Under-
takings."

The Gentle Reader feels that whatever may be
the merits of Gondibert, Sir William Davenant
is a gallant gentleman and worthy of his lasting
friendship.

The Gentle Reader has a warm place in his
heart for those whom he calls the paradisaical
writers.   These are the unfallen spirits who reveal
their native dispositions and are not ashamed.
They write about that which they find most interesting — themselves.   They not only tell us what
happens, but what they think and how they feel.
We are made partners of their joys and sorrows.
The first person singular is glorified by their use.

"But," says the Severe Moralist, "don't you frequently discover that these persons are vain?"

"Precisely so," answers the Gentle Reader, "and that's what I want to find out. How are you going to discover what an author thinks about himself if he hides behind a mask of impersonality? There is no getting acquainted with such hypocrites. In five hundred pages you may not have a glimpse of the man behind the book, though he may be bubbling over with self-conceit. There was Alexander Cruden, one of the most eccentric persons of the eighteenth century. Fully persuaded of his own greatness, he called himself Alexander the Corrector and announced that he was destined to be 'the second Joseph and a great man at court.' He haunted the ante-chambers of the nobility, but found only one nobleman who would listen to him, Earl Paulett, 'who being goutish in his feet could not run away from the Corrector as other men are apt to do.' Cruden appears to have spent his leisure moments in going about London with a large piece of sponge with which he erased any offensive chalk marks on the walls. 'This employment,' says his biographer, 'occasionally

made his walks very tedious.' Now one might
consult Cruden's 'Concordance of the Holy
Scriptures' in vain for any hint of these idiosyn-
crasies of the author. Perhaps the nature of the
work made this impossible. But what shall we
say of writers who, having no such excuse, take
pains to conceal from us what manner of men
they were. Even David Hume, whose good opinion of himself is a credit to his critical sagacity,
assumes an apologetic tone when he ventures upon
a sketch of his own life. 'It is difficult,' he
says, 'for a man to speak long about himself
without vanity; therefore I shall be brief.' What
obtuseness that shows in a philosopher who actually wrote a treatise on human nature! What
did he know about human nature if he thought
anybody would read an auto-biography that was
without vanity? Vanity is one of the most lovable of weaknesses. If in our contemporaries it
sometimes troubles us, that is only because two
bodies cannot occupy the same space at the same
time. But when it is all put in a book and the
pure juices of self-satisfaction have been allowed
to mellow for a few centuries, nothing can be
more delicious."

His heart was won by a single sentence in one of Horace Walpole's letters: "I write to you as I think." To the writer who gives him this mark of confidence he is as faithful as is the Arab to the guest who has eaten salt in his tent. The books which contain the results of thought are common enough, but it is a rare privilege to share with a pleasant gentleman the act of thinking. If the thoughts are those which arise spontaneously out of the incidents of the passing day, so much the better. He therefore warmly resents Wordsworth's remark about "that cold and false-hearted, frenchified coxcomb, Horace Walpole."

"What has Horace Walpole done except to give us a picture of his own disposition and incidentally of the world he lived in? It is an instance of the ingratitude of Republics — and the Republic of Letters is the most ungrateful of them all — that this should be made the ground of a railing accusation against him. Walpole might answer as Timoleon did, when, after having restored the liberties of Syracuse, a citizen denounced him in the popular assembly. The Liberator replied: 'I cannot sufficiently express

my gratitude to the gods for granting my request
in permitting me to see all the Syracusans enjoy
the liberty of saying what they think fit.' A man
who could write letters for sixty-two years re-
vealing every phase of feeling for the benefit of
posterity earns the right of making as magnanimous a retort as that of any of Plutarch's men.
He might well thank the gods for permitting
him to furnish future generations with ample
material for passing judgment upon him. For
myself, I do not agree with Wordsworth. I have
summered and wintered with Horace Walpole
and he has never played me false; he has shown
himself exactly as he is. To be sure, he has his
weaknesses, but he is always ready to share them
with his friends. I suppose that is the reason
why he is accused of being frenchified. A true
born Englishman would have kept his faults to
himself as if they were incommunicable attri-
butes. I am not going to allow a bit of criticism
to come between us at this late day. The relation between Reader and Author is not to be
treated so lightly. I believe that there is no
reason for separation in such cases except incom-
patibility of temper."

Then he makes his way to Strawberry Hill
and listens to its master describing his possession. "It is set in enameled meadows with
filigree hedges, —

> 'A small Euphrates through the piece is rolled
> And little finches wave their wings of gold.'

Two delightful roads, that you would call dusty,
supply me continually with coaches and chaises;
barges as solemn as barons of the exchequer move
under my window; Richmond Hill and Ham
Walks bound my prospects; but thank God!
the Thames is between me and the Duchess of
Queensberry. Dowagers as plenty as flounders
inhabit all around; and Pope's ghost is just now
skimming under my window by a most poetical
moonlight."

It is pleasant to sit in the Gothic villa on
Strawberry Hill and see the world pass by. The
small Euphrates, the filigree hedges, and the
gossiping dowagers, being in the foreground,
appear more important than they do in the formal histories which have no perspective. But
the great world does pass by, and the master of
the house is familiar with it and recognizes every

important person in the procession. Was he not
a Prime Minister's son, and were not his first
letters written from Downing Street?

How rapidly the procession moves, giving only
time for a nod and a word! The reader is like
a country cousin in the metropolis bewildered
by a host of new sensations. Now and then he
smiles as some one whose name has been long
familiar is pointed out. The chief wonder is
that there are so many notabilities of whom he
has never heard before. What an unconscion-
able number of Duchesses there are, and each one
has a history! How different the Statesmen are
from what he had imagined; not nearly so wise
but ever so much more amusing. Even the great
William Pitt appears to be only "Sir William
Quixote," and a fantastic figure he is! Strawberry Hill has its prejudices. It listens incredu-
lously to the stories illustrative of incorruptible
political virtue. They are tales to be told to
Posterity.

In regard to the historical drama that unfolds
there is a pleasant ambiguity. Which is it that
sees behind the scenes, — the writer or the present-
day reader? The reader representing Posterity

has a general notion of the progress of events.
He thinks he knows how things actually came
out and which were the more important.  He is
anxious to know how they strike a contemporary.
But he is chastened by the discovery of the in-
numerable incidents which Posterity has forgotten, but which made a great stir in their day.
" The Tower guns have sworn through thick and
thin that Prince Ferdinand has entirely demol-
ished the French, and city bonfires all believe it."
Prince Ferdinand " is the most fashionable man
in England.  Have not the Tower guns and all
the parsons in London been ordered to pray for
him ? "

The Gentle Reader is almost tempted to look
up Prince Ferdinand, but is diverted from this
inquiry by a bit of gossip about the Duke of
Marlborough and the silver spoons.

When he comes to the glorious year 1775 he
is eager to learn the sensations of Walpole when
the echoes of the " shot heard round the world "
come to him.  The shot is heard, but its effect
is not so startling as might have been imagined.
" I did but put my head into London on Thurs-
day, and more bad news from America.  I won-

der when it will be bad enough to make folks think it so, without going on?" Then Walpole turns to something more interesting. " I have a great mind to tell you a Twickenham story."

It is about a certain Captain Mawhood who had " applied himself to learn the classics and free-thinking and was always disputing with the parson of the parish about Dido and his own soul."

It is not just what the Gentle Reader was expecting, but he adapts himself cheerfully to the situation.

" I was about to inquire what you thought about the American war, but we may come to that at some other time. Now let us have the Twickenham story."


The Gentle Reader loves the writers who reveal their intellectual limitations, but he does not care for those who insist upon telling him their physical ailments. He is averse to the letters and journals which are merely contributions to pathology. Indeed, he would, if he had his own way, allow the mention of only one malady, the gout. This is doubtless painful enough in the flesh, but

in a book it has many pleasant associations. Its
intervals seem conducive to reminiscence, and its
twinges are the occasions of eloquent objurga-
tions which light up many an otherwise colorless
page.

With all his tolerance of vanity he dislikes
that inverted kind which induces certain morbid
persons to write out painful confessions of their
own sins.  He is willing to believe that they are
far from perfect, but he is sceptical in regard to
their claims to be the chief of sinners.  It is
hard to attain distinction in a line where there is
so much competition.

When he finds a book of Life and Letters
unreadable, he does not bring a railing accusation against either the biographer or the biogra-
phee.

They may both have been interesting persons,
though the result in cold print is not exhilarating.  He knows how volatile is the charm of
personality, and how hard it is to preserve the
best things.  His friend, who is a great diner-
out, says : " Those were delightful people I met
at dinner yesterday, and what a capital story the
judge told !  I laugh every time I think about it."

"What story?" asks the Gentle Reader, eager for the crumbs that fall from the witty man's table.

"I can't remember just what it was about, or what was the point of it; but it was a good story, and you would have thought so, too, if you had heard the judge tell it."

"I certainly should," replies the Gentle Reader, "and I shall always believe, on your testimony, that the judge is one of the best story-tellers in existence."

In like manner he believes in interesting things that great men must have done which unfortunately were not taken down by any one at the time.

The Gentle Reader himself is not much at home in fashionable literary society. He is a shy person, and his embarrassment is increased by the consciousness that he seldom gets round to a book till after people are through talking about it. Not that he prides himself on this fact; for he is far from cherishing the foolish prejudice against new books.

"'David Copperfield' was a new book once,

and it was as good then as it is now." It simply happens that there are so many good books that it is hard to keep up with the procession. Besides, he has discovered that the books that are talked about can be talked about just as well without being read; this leaves him more time for his old favorites.

" I have a sweet little story for you," says the charming authoress. " I am sure you like sweet little stories."

" Only one lump, if you please," says the Gentle Reader.

In spite of his genial temperament there are some subjects on which he is intolerant. When he picks up a story that turns out to be only a Tract for the Times, he turns indignantly on the author.

" Sirrah," he cries, under the influence of deep feeling, relapsing into the vernacular of romance, "you gained access to me under the plea that you were going to please me; and now that you have stolen a portion of my time, you throw off all disguise, and admit that you entered with intent to instruct, and that you do not care whether you please me or not! I've a mind to have you

arrested for obtaining my attention under false
pretenses! How villainously we are imposed
upon! Only the other day a man came to me
highly recommended as an architect. I employed
him to build me a Castle in Spain, regardless of
expense. When I suggested a few pleasant embellishments, the wretch refused on the ground
that he never saw anything of the kind in the
town he came from, — Toledo, Ohio. If he had
pleaded honest poverty of invention I should
have forgiven him, but he took a high and mighty
tone with me, and said that it was against his
principles to allow any incident that was not
probable. 'Who said that it should be probable?' I replied. 'It is your business to make
it *seem* probable.'"

He highly disapproves of what he considers
the cheese-paring economy on the part of certain
novelists in the endowment of their characters.
"Their traits are so microscopic, and require
such minute analysis, that I get half through the
book before I know which is which. It seems as
if the writers were not sure that there was enough
human nature to go around. They should study
the good old story of Aboukir and Abousir.

" ' There were in the city of Alexandria two men, — one was a dyer, and his name was Aboukir; the other was a barber, and his name was Abousir. They were neighbors, and the dyer was a swindler, a liar, and a person of exceeding wickedness.'

" Now, there the writer and reader start fair. There are no unnecessary concealments. You know that the dyer is a villain, and you are on your guard. You are not told in the first paragraph about the barber, but you take it for granted that he is an excellent, well-meaning man, who is destined to become enormously wealthy. And so it turns out. If our writers would only follow this straightforward method we should hear less about nervous prostration among the reading classes." He is very severe on the whimsical notion, that never occurred to any one until the last century, of saying that the heroine is not beautiful.

" Such a remark is altogether gratuitous. When I become attached to a young lady in fiction she always appears to me to be an extraordinarily lovely creature. It's sheer impertinence for the author to intrude, every now and then, just to call my attention to the fact that her complexion is not good, and that her features are irregular. It's bad manners, — and, besides, I don't believe that it's true."

Nothing, however, so offends the Gentle Reader as the trick of elaborating a plot and then refusing to elucidate it, and leaving everything at loose ends. He feels toward this misdirected ingenuity as Miss Edgeworth's Harry did toward the conundrum which his sister proposed.

" This is quite different," he said, " from the others. The worst of it is that after laboring ever so hard at one riddle it does not in the least lead to another. The next is always on some other principle."

" Yes, to be sure," said Lucy. " Nobody who knows how to puzzle would give two riddles of the same kind; that would be too easy."

" But then, without something to guide one," said Harry, " there is no getting on."

" Not in your regular way," said Lucy.

" That is the very thing I complain of," said Harry.

" Complain! But my dear Harry, riddles are meant only to divert one."

"But they do not divert me," said Harry; "they only puzzle me."

The Gentle Reader is inclined to impute unworthy motives to the writer whose work merely puzzles him.

"The lazy unscrupulous fellow takes a job, and then throws it up and leaves me to finish it for him. It's a clear breach of contract! That sort of thing would never have been allowed in any well-governed community. Fancy what would have happened in the court of Shahriar, where story-telling was taken seriously."

Sheherazade has got Sindbad on the moving island.

"How did he get off?" asks the Sultan.

"That's for your majesty to find out," answers Sheherazade archly. "Maybe he got off, and maybe he did n't. That's the problem."

"Off with her head!" says the Sultan.

When sore beset by novelists who, under the guise of fiction, attempt to saddle him with "the weary weight of all this unintelligible world," the Gentle Reader takes refuge with one who has never deceived him.

"What shall it be?" says Sir Walter.

" As you please, Sir Walter."

" No!   As *you* please, Gentle Reader.  If you have nothing else in mind, how would this do for a start? —

> ' Waken! Lords and Ladies gay!
> On the mountain dawns the day.'

It 's a fine morning, and it 's a gallant company! Let 's go with them!"

" Let 's!" cries the Gentle Reader.

# The Enjoyment of Poetry

❧

**B**ROWNING'S description of the effect of the recital of classic poetry upon a band of piratical Greeks must seem to many persons to be exaggerated : —

> " Then, because Greeks are Greeks, and hearts are hearts,
>   And poetry is power, they all outbroke
>   In a great joyous laughter with much love."

Because Americans are Americans, and business is business, and time is money, and life is earnest, we take our poetry much more seriously than that. We are ready to form classes to study it and to discuss it, but these solemn assemblies are not likely to be disturbed by outbursts of " great joyous laughter."

We usually accept poetry as mental discipline. It is as if the poet said, " Go to, now. I will

produce a masterpiece." Thereupon the conscientious reader answers, "Very well; I can stand
it. I will apply myself with all diligence, that
by means of it I may improve my mind." Who
has not sometimes quailed before the long row of
British Poets in uniform binding, standing stiffly
side by side, like so many British grenadiers on
dress parade? Who has not felt his courage ooze
away at the sight of those melancholy volumes
labeled Complete Poetical Works? Poetical Remains they used to call them, and there is something funereal in their aspect.

The old hymn says, "Religion never was de-
signed to make our pleasures less," and the same
thing ought to be said about poetry. The dis-
taste for poetry arises largely from the habit of
treating it as if it were only a more difficult kind
of prose. We are so much under the tyranny of
the scientific method that the habits of the school-
room intrude, and we try to extract instruction
from what was meant to give us joy. The prosaic
commentary obscures the beauty of the text, so
that

"The glad old romance, the gay chivalrous story,
    With its fables of faery, its legends of glory,

> Is turned to a tedious instruction, not new,
> To the children, who read it insipidly through."

One of the most ruthless invasions of the prosaic faculties into the realm of poetry comes from the thirst for general information. When this thirst becomes a disease, it is not satisfied with census reports and encyclopædia articles, but values literature according to the number of facts presented. Suppose these lines from " Paradise Lost " to be taken for study : —

> " Thick as autumnal leaves that strow the brooks
> In Vallombrosa, where th' Etrurian shades
> High over-arched embower, or scattered sedge
> Afloat, when with fierce winds Orion armed
> Hath vexed the Red Sea coast, whose waves o'erthrew
> Busiris and his Memphian chivalry."

What an opportunity this presents to the schoolmaster ! " Come now," he cries with pedagogic glee, " answer me a few questions. Where is Vallombrosa ? What is the character of its autumnal foliage ? Bound Etruria. What is sedge ? Explain the myth of Orion ? Point out the constellation on the map of the heavens. Where is the Red Sea ? Who was Busiris ? By what other name was he known ? Who were the Memphian Chivalry ? "

Here is material for exhaustive research in geography, ancient and modern, history, botany, astronomy, meteorology, chronology, and archæology. The industrious student may get almost as much information out of "Paradise Lost" as from one of those handy compilations of useful knowledge, which are sold on the railway cars for twenty-five cents. As for the poetry of Milton, that is another matter.

Next to the temptation to use a poem as a receptacle for a mass of collateral information is that to use it for the display of one's own penetration. As in the one case it is treated as if it were an encyclopædia article, in the other it is treated as if it were a verbal puzzle. It is taken for granted that the intention of the poet is to conceal thought, and the game is for the reader to find it out. We are hunting for hidden meanings, and we greet one another with the grim salutation of the creatures in the jungle: "Good hunting!" "What is the meaning of this passage?" Who has not heard this sudden question propounded in regard to the most transparent sentence from an author who is deemed worthy of study? The uninitiated, in the simplicity of his heart, might answer that he probably means what he says. Not at all; if that were so, " what are we here for?" We are here to find hidden meanings, and one who finds the meaning simple must be stopped, as Armado stops Moth, with

"Define, define, well-educated infant."

It is a verbal masquerade to which we have been invited. No knowing what princes in disguise, as well as anarchists and nihilists and other objectionably interesting persons, may be discovered when the time for unmasking comes.

Now, the effect of all this is that many persons turn away from the poets altogether. Why should they spend valuable time in trying to unravel the meaning of lines which were invented to baffle them? There are plenty of things we do not understand, without going out of our way to find them. Then, as Pope observes,

"True No-meaning puzzles more than Wit."

The poets themselves, as if conscious that they are objects of suspicion, are inclined to be apologetic, and endeavor to show that they are doing business on a sound prosaic basis. Wordsworth set the example of such painstaking self-justification. His conscience compelled him to make amends to the literal minded Public for poetic indiscretions, and to offer to settle all claims for damages. What a shame-faced excuse he makes for the noble lines on Rob Roy's grave. " I have since been told that I was misinformed as to the burial-place of Rob Roy; if so, I may plead in excuse that I wrote on apparently good authority, namely that of a well-educated lady who lived at the head of the lake."

One is reminded of the preface to the works of The Sweet Singer of Michigan : " This little book is composed of truthful pieces. All those which speak of being killed, died, or drowned are truthful songs, others are more truth than poetry."

It is against this mistaken conscientiousness that the Gentle Reader protests. He insists that the true " defense of poesy " is that it has an altogether different function from prose. It is not to be appreciated by the prosaic understanding; unless, indeed, that awkward faculty be

treated to some Delsartean decomposing exercises to get rid of its stiffness.

"When I want more truth than poetry," he
says, "I will go directly to The Sweet Singer of
Michigan, or I will inquire of the well-educated
lady who lives at the head of the lake.   I do not
like to have a poet troubled about such small
matters."

Then he reads with approval the remarks of
one of his own order who lived in the seventeenth
century, who protests against those "who take
away the liberty of a poet and fetter his feet in
the shackles of an historian.   For why should a
poet doubt in story to mend the intrigues of
fortune by more delightful conveyances of probable fictions because austere historians have entered into bond to truth; an obligation which
were in poets as foolish and unnecessary as is
the bondage of false martyrs, who lie in chains
for a mistaken opinion.   But by this I would
imply that truth, narrative and past, is the idol
of historians (who worship a dead thing), and
truth operative and by effects continually alive is
the mistress of poets, who hath not her existence
in matter but in reason."

I am well aware that the attitude of the Gentle Reader seems to many strenuous persons to be unworthy of our industrial civilization. These persons insist that we shall make hard work of our poetry, if for no other reason than to preserve our self-respect. Here as elsewhere they insist upon the stern law that if a man will not labor neither shall he eat. Even the poems of an earlier and simpler age which any child can understand must be invested with some artificial difficulty. The learned guardians of these treasures insist that they cannot be appreciated unless there has been much preliminary wrestling with a "critical apparatus," and much delving among "original sources." This is the same principle that makes the prudent householder provide a sharp saw and a sufficient pile of cord wood as a test to be applied to the stranger who asks for a breakfast. There is much academic disapproval of one who in defiance of all law insists on enjoying poetry after his own "undressed, unpolished, uneducated, unpruned, untrained, or rather unlettered, or ratherest unconfirmed fashion." I, however, so thoroughly sympathize with the Gentle Reader that I desire to present his point of view.

To understand poetry is a vain ambition. That which we fully understand is the part that is *not* poetry. It is that which passes our understanding which has the secret in itself. There is an incommunicable grace that defies all attempts at analysis. Poetry is like music; it is fitted, not to define an idea or to describe a fact, but to voice a mood. The mood may be the mood of a very simple person, — the mood of a shepherd watching his flocks, or of a peasant in the fields; or, on the other hand, it may be the mood of a philosopher whose mind has been engrossed with the most subtle problems of existence. But in each case the mood, by some suggestion, must be communicated to us. Thoughts and facts must be transfigured; they must come to us as through some finer medium. As we are told that we must experience religion before we know what religion is, so we must experience poetry. The poet is the enchanter, and we are the willing victims of his spells: —

> " Would'st thou see
> A man i' th' clouds and hear him speak to thee?
> Would'st thou be in a dream and yet not sleep?
> Or would'st thou in a moment laugh and weep?

Wouldest thou lose thyself and catch no harm?
And find thyself again without a charm?

. . . . . . . . . . .

O then come hither
And lay my book, thy head and heart together."

Only the reader who yields to the charm can
dream the dream. The poet may weave his story
of the most common stuff, but "there's magic in
the web of it." If we are conscious of this magi-
cal power, we forgive the lack of everything else.
The poet may be as ignorant as Aladdin himself,
but he has a strange power over our imaginations. At his word they obey, traversing conti-
nents, building palaces, painting pictures. They
say, "We are ready to obey as thy slaves, and
the slaves of all that have that lamp in their
hands, — we and the other slaves of the lamp."

This is the characteristic of the poet's power.
He does not construct a work of the imagination, — he makes our imaginations do that. That
is why the fine passages of elaborate description
in verse are usually failures. The verse-maker
describes accurately and at length. The poet
speaks a word, and Presto! change! We are
transported into a new land, and our eyes are
"baptized into the grace and privilege of see-

ing." Many have taken in hand to write descriptions of spring; and some few painstaking persons have nerved themselves to read what has been written. I turn to the prologue of the "Canterbury Tales;" it is not about spring, it is spring, and I am among those who long to go upon a pilgrimage. A description of a jungle is an impertinence to one who has come under the spell of William Blake's

> "Tiger! tiger! burning bright
> In the forest of the night."

Those fierce eyes glowing there in the darkness sufficiently illuminate the scene. Immediately it is midsummer, and we feel all its delicious languor when Browning's David sings of

> "The sleep in the dried river-channel where bulrushes tell
> That the water was wont to go warbling so softly and well."

The first essential to the enjoyment of poetry is leisure. The demon Hurry is the tempter, and knowledge is the forbidden fruit in the poet's paradise. To enjoy poetry, you must renounce not only your easily besetting sins, but your easily besetting virtues as well. You must not be industrious, or argumentative, or conscientious, or strenuous. I do not mean that you must be a person of unlimited leisure and without visible means of support. I have known some very conscientious students of literature who, when off duty, found time to enjoy poetry. I mean that if you have only half an hour for poetry, for that half hour you must be in a leisurely frame of mind.

The poet differs from the novelist in that he requires us to rest from our labors. The ordinary novel is easy reading, because it takes us as we are, in the midst of our hurry. The mind has been going at express speed all the day; what the novelist does is to turn the switch, and off we go on another track. The steam is up, and the wheels go around just the same. The great thing is still action, and we eagerly turn the pages to see what is going to happen next, — unless we are reading some of our modern realistic studies of character. Even then we are lured on by the expectation that, at the last moment, something may happen. But when we turn to the poets, we are in the land of the lotus-eaters. The atmosphere is that of a perfect day,

"Whereon it is enough for me
Not to be doing, but to be."

Into this land our daily cares cannot follow us.
It is an

> " enchanted land, we know not where,
> But lovely as a landscape in a dream."

Once in this enchanted country, haste seems
foolish. Why should we toil on as if we were
walking for a wager? It is as if one had the
privilege of joining Izaak Walton as he loiters
in the cool shade of a sweet honeysuckle hedge,
and should churlishly trudge on along the dusty
highway rather than accept the gentle angler's
invitation : " Pray, let us rest ourselves in this
sweet, shady arbor of jessamine and myrtle ; and
I will requite you with a bottle of sack, and when
you have pledged me, I will repeat the verses I
promised you." One may, as a matter of strict
conscience, be both a pedestrian and a prohibi-
tionist, and yet not find it in his heart to decline
such an invitation.

The poets who delight us with their verses are
not always serious-minded persons with an important thought to communicate. When I read,

> " In Xanadu did Kubla Khan
> A stately pleasure-dome decree,"

I am not a bit wiser than I was before, but I am

a great deal happier; although I have not the slightest idea where Xanadu was, and only the vaguest notion of Kubla Khan.

There are poems whose charm lies in their illusiveness. Fancy any one trying to explain Rossetti's "Blessed Damozel." Yet when the mood is on us we see her as she leans

> "From the gold bar of Heaven:
> Her eyes were deeper than the depth
> Of waters stilled at even;
> She had three lilies in her hand
> And the stars in her hair were seven."

We look over the mystic ramparts and are dimly conscious that

> "the souls mounting up to God
> Went by her like thin flames."

This is not astronomy nor theology, nor any of the things we know all about — it is only poetry.

Let no one trouble me by attempting to elucidate "Childe Roland to the Dark Tower came." I do not care for a Baedeker. I prefer to lose my way. I love the darkness rather than light. I do not care for a topographical chart of the hills that

> "like giants at a hunting lay,
> Chin upon hand."

The mood in which we enjoy such poetry is that described in Emerson's "Forerunners."

> " Long I followed happy guides,
> I could never reach their sides.
>
> . . . . . .
>
> But no speed of mine avails
> To hunt upon their shining trails.
>
> . . . . . .
>
> On eastern hills I see their smokes,
> Mixed with mist by distant lochs.
> I met many travelers
> Who the road had surely kept :
> They saw not my fine revelers."

If our thoughts make haste to join these " fine revelers," rejoicing in the sense of freedom and mystery, delighting in the mist and the wind, careless of attaining so that we may follow the shining trails, all is well.

As there are poems which are not meant to be understood, so there are poems that are not meant to be read ; that is, to be read through. There is Keats's " Endymion," for instance. I have never been able to get on with it. Yet it is delightful, — that is the very reason why I do not care to get on with it. Wherever I begin, I feel that I might as well stay where I am. It is a sweet wilderness into which the reader is introduced.

> " Paths there were many,
> Winding through palmy fern and rushes fenny
> And ivy banks ; all leading pleasantly
> To a wide lawn.  . . .
>                     Who could tell
> The freshness of the space of heaven above,
> Edged round with dark tree-tops ? — through which a dove
> Would often beat its wings, and often, too,
> A little cloud would move across the blue."

We are brought into the very midst of this pleasantness.  Deep in the wood we see fair faces and
garments white.  We see the shepherds coming
to the woodland altar.

> " A crowd of shepherds with as sunburnt looks
> As may be read of in Arcadian books;
> Such as sat list'ning round Apollo's pipe
> When the great deity, for earth too ripe,
> Let his divinity o'erflowing die
> In music, through the vales of Thessaly."

We see the venerable priest pouring out the
sweet-scented wine, and then we see the young
Endymion himself : —

> " He seemed
> To common lookers-on like one who dreamed
> Of idleness in groves Elysian."

What happened next?  What did Endymion
do?  Really, I do not know.  It is so much
pleasanter, at this point, to close the book, and

dream " of idleness in groves Elysian." The
chances are that when one turns to the poem
again he will not begin where he left off, but at
the beginning, and read as if he had never read
it before ; or rather, with more enjoyment because
he has read it so many times : —

> " A thing of beauty is a joy forever :
>   Its loveliness increases ; it will never
>   Pass into nothingness ; but still will keep
>   A bower quiet for us, and a sleep
>   Full of sweet dreams, and health, and quiet breathing."

Shelley describes a mood such as Keats brings
to us : —

> " My spirit like a charmèd bark doth swim
>   Upon the liquid waves of thy sweet singing
>   Far away into regions dim
>   Of rapture, as a boat with swift sails winging
>   Its way adown some many-winding river."

He who finds himself afloat upon the " many-
winding river " throws aside the laboring oar. It
is enough to float on, — he cares not whither.

What greater pleasure is there than in the
" Idylls of the King " provided we do not study
them, but dream them. We must enter into the
poet's own mood : —

> " I seemed
> To sail with Arthur under looming shores,
> Point after point, till on to dawn, when dreams
> Begin to feel the truth and stir of day."

It is good to be there, in that far-off time, good to come to Camelot : —

> " Built by old kings, age after age,
> So strange and rich and dim."

All we see of kings, and magicians, and ladies, and knights is "strange and rich and dim." Over everything is a luminous haze. There are

> " hollow tramplings up and down,
> And muffled voices heard, and shadows past."

There is the flashing of swords, the weaving of spells, the seeing of visions. All these things become real to us ; not simply the stainless king and the sinful queen, the prowess of Lancelot and the love of Elaine, but the magic of Merlin and the sorceries of Vivien, with her charms

> " Of woven paces and of waving hands."

And we must stand at last with King Arthur on the shore of the mystic sea, and see the barge come slowly with the three queens, " black-stoled, black-hooded, like a dream ; " and hear across the water a cry,

"As it were one voice, an agony
Of lamentation, like a wind that shrills
All night in a waste land, where no one comes,
Or hath come, since the making of the world."

But what good is there in all this? Why waste
time on idle dreams? We hear Walt Whitman's
challenge to romantic poetry: —

"Arthur vanished with all his knights, Merlin and Lancelot
   and Galahad, all gone, dissolved utterly like an ex-
   halation;
Embroidered, dazzling, foreign world, with all its gorgeous
   legends, myths,
Its kings and castles proud, its priests and warlike lords and
   courtly dames,
Passed to its charnel vault, coffined with crown and armor on,
Blazoned with Shakspere's purple page
And dirged by Tennyson's sweet sad rhyme."

Away with the old romance! Make room for the
modern bard, who is

"Bluffed not a bit by drain-pipes, gasometers, and artificial
   fertilizers."

The Gentle Reader, also, is not to be bluffed by
any useful things, however unpleasant they may
be, but he winces a little as he reads that the
" far superber themes for poets and for art " in-
clude the teaching by the poet of how

" To use the hammer and the saw (rip or cross-cut),
  To cultivate a turn for carpentering, plastering, painting,
  To work as tailor, tailoress, nurse, hostler, porter,
  To invent a little something ingenious to aid the washing,
      cooking, cleaning."

The Muse of Poetry shrieks at the mighty lines in praise of " leather-dressing, coach-making, boiler-making," and the rest. Boiler-making, she protests, is a useful industry and highly to be commended, but it is not music. When asked to give a reason why she should not receive all these things as poetry, the Muse is much embarrassed. " It 's all true," she says. " Leather-dressing and boiler-making are undoubted realities, while Arthur and Lancelot may be myths." Yet she is not quite ready to be off with the old love and on with the new, — it 's all so sudden.

Whitman himself furnishes the best illustrations of the difference between poetry and prose. He comes like another Balaam to prophesy against those who associate poetry with beauty of form and melody of words ; and then the poetic spirit seizes upon him and lifts him into the region of harmony. In the Song of the Universal he declares that —

" From imperfection's murkiest cloud
    Darts always forth one ray of perfect light,
    One flash of heaven's glory.
    To fashion's, customs discord,
    To the mad Babel's din, the deafening orgies,
    Soothing each lull, a strain is heard, just heard
    From some far shore, the final chorus sounding.
    O the blest eyes, the happy hearts
    That see, that know the guiding thread so fine
    Along the mighty labyrinth."

There speaks the poet declaring the true faith,
which except a man believe he is condemned
everlastingly to the outer darkness. His task
is selective. No matter about the murki-
ness of the cloud he must make us see the
ray of perfect light. In the mad Babel-din he
must hear and repeat the strain of pure music.
As to the field of choice, it may be as wide as
the world, but he must choose as a poet, and not
after the manner of the man with the muck-rake.

" In this broad earth of ours
    Amid the measureless grossness and the slag,
    Inclosed and safe within the central heart
    Nestles the seed perfection."

When the poet delves in the grossness and the
slag, he does so as one engaged in the search for
the perfect.

"My feeling," says the Gentle Reader, "about the proper material for poetry, is very much like that of Whitman in regard to humanity —

'When warrantee deeds loafe in chairs opposite, and are my
      friendly companions,
I intend to reach them my hand and make as much of them as
  ·     I do of men and women like you.'

"So I say, when drain pipes and cross-cut saws and the beef on the butcher's stalls are invested with beautiful associations and thrill my soul in some mysterious fashion, then I will make as much of these things as I do of the murmuring pines and the hemlocks. When a poet makes bank clerks and stevedores and wood-choppers to loom before my imagination in heroic proportions, I will receive them as I do the heroes of old. But, mind you, the miracle must be actually performed; I will not be put off with a prospectus."

Now and then the miracle is performed. We are made to feel the romance that surrounds the American pioneer, we hear the

"Crackling blows of axes sounding musically, driven by strong
      arms."

But, for the most part, Whitman, when under

the influence of deep feeling, forgets his theory, and uses as his symbols those things which have already been invested with poetical associations. Turn to that marvelous dirge, "When Lilacs last in the Dooryard bloomed." There is here no catalogue of facts or events, no parade of glaring realism. Tennyson's "sweet sad rhyme" has nowhere more delicious music than we find in the measured cadence of these lines. We are not told the news of the assassination of Lincoln as a man on the street might tell it. It comes to us through suggestion. We are made to feel a mood, not to listen to the description of an event. There is symbolism, suggestion, color, mystery. We inhale the languorous fragrance of the lilacs; we see the drooping star; in secluded recesses we hear "a shy and hidden bird" warbling a song; there are dim-lit churches and shuddering organs and tolling bells, and there is one soul heart-broken, seeing all and hearing all.

"Comrades mine and I in the midst, and their memory ever to keep, for the dead I loved so well,
For the sweetest, wisest soul of all my days and lands — and this for his dear sake,
Lilac and star and bird twined with the chant of my soul,
There in the fragrant pines and the cedars dusk and dim."

This is real poetry, and yet while we yield to the charm we are conscious that it is made up of the old familiar elements.

Tennyson's apology to a utilitarian age was not needed : —

> " Perhaps some modern touches here and there
> Redeemed it from the charge of nothingness."

The " modern touches " we can spare. The modern life we have always with us; but it is a rare privilege to enjoy the best things of the past. It is the poet who is the minister of this fine grace. The historian tells us what men of the past did, the philosopher tells us how their civilizations developed and decayed ; we smile at their superstitions, and pride ourselves upon our progress. But the ethereal part has vanished, that which made their very superstitions beautiful and cast a halo over their struggles. These are the elements out of which the poet creates his world, into which we may enter. In the order of historic development chivalry must give way before democracy, and loyalty to the king must fade before the increasing sense of liberty and equality; but the highest ideals of chivalry may remain. Imaginative and romantic poetry has this high mission to preserve what otherwise would be lost. It lifts the mind above the daily routine into the region of pure joy. Whatever necessary changes take place in the world we find, in

> " All lovely tales which we have heard or read,
> An endless fountain of immortal drink,
> Pouring unto us from the heaven's brink."

I have said that one may be a true poet without having any very important thought to communicate, but it must be said that most of the great poets have been serious thinkers as well. They have had their philosophy of life, their thoughts about nature and about human duty and destiny. It is the function of the poet not only to create for us an ideal world and to fill it with ideal creatures, but also to reveal to us the ideal element in the actual world.

" I do not know what poetical is," says Audrey. " Is it honest in deed and word ? Is it a true thing ? " We must not answer with Touchstone : " No, truly ! for the truest poetry is the most feigning."

The poetical interpretation of the world is not

feigning; it is a true thing, — the truest thing of which we can know. The grace and sublimity which we see through the poet's eyes are real. We must, however, still insist on our main contention. The poet, if he is to hold us, must always be a poet. His thought must be in solution, and not appear as a dull precipitate of prose. He may be philosophical, but he must not philosophize. He may be moral, but he must not moralize. He may be religious, but let him spare his homilies.

"Whatever the philosopher saith should be done," said Sir Philip Sidney; "the peerless poet giveth a perfect picture of it. He yieldeth to the power of the mind an image of that of which the philosopher bestoweth but a wordish description. . . . The poet doth not only show the way, but doth give so sweet a prospect unto the way as will entice any man to enter it. Nay, he doth as if your journey should lie through a fair vineyard, at first give you a cluster of grapes."

We have a right to ask our poets to be pleasant companions even when they discourse on the highest themes. Even when they have theories

of their own about what we should enjoy, let us
not allow them to foist upon us " wordish descriptions " of excellent things instead of poetry.
When the poet invites me to go with him I first
ask, " Let me taste your grapes."

You remember Mr. By-ends in the " Pilgrim's
Progress," — how he said of Christian and Hopeful, " They are headstrong men who think it their
duty to rush on in their journey in all weathers,
while I am for waiting for wind or tide.  I am
for Religion when he walks in his silver slippers
in the sunshine."   That was very reprehensible
in Mr. By-ends, and he richly deserved the rebuke which was afterward administered to him.
But when we change the subject, and speak, not
of religion, but of poetry, I confess that I am
very much of Mr. By-ends' way of thinking.
There are literary Puritans who, when they take
up the study of a poet, make it a point of conscience to go on to the bitter end of his poetical
works.  If they start with Wordsworth on his
" Excursion," they trudge on in all weathers.
They *do* the poem, as when going abroad they do
Europe in six weeks.   As the revival hymn says,
" doing is a deadly thing."   Let me say, good

Christian and Hopeful, that though I admire
your persistence, I cannot accompany you. I
am for a poet only when he puts on his singing
robes and walks in the sunshine. As for those
times when he goes on prosing in rhyme from
force of habit, I think it is more respectful as
well as more pleasurable to allow him to walk
alone.

Shelley's definition of poetry as "the record of
the best and happiest moments of the happiest
and best minds" suggests the whole duty of the
reader. All that is required of him is to obey
the Golden Rule. There must be perfect reciprocity and fraternal sympathy. The poet, being
human, has his unhappy hours, when all things
are full of labor. Upon such hours the Gentle
Reader does not intrude. In their happiest moments they meet as if by chance. In this encounter they are pleased with one another and
with the world they live in. How could it be
otherwise? It is indeed a wonderful world, transfigured in the light of thought. Familiar objects
lose their sharp outlines and become symbols of
universal realities. Likenesses, before unthought

of, appear. Nature becomes a mirror of the soul, and answers instantly to each passing mood. Words are no longer chosen, they come unbidden as the poet and his reader

> " mount to Paradise
> By the stairway of surprise."

# The Mission of Humor

❦

IN " The Last Tournament " we are told how

"Dagonet, the fool, whom Gawain in his moods
Had made mock-knight of Arthur's Table Round,
At Camelot, high above the yellowing woods,
Danced like a withered leaf before the hall."

That is the view which many worthy people take of the humorist. He is Sir Dagonet. Among the serious persons who are doing the useful work of the world, discovering its laws, classifying its facts, forecasting its future, this light-minded, light-hearted creature comes with his untimely jests. In their idle moments they tolerate the mock-knight, but when important business is on hand they dismiss him, as did Sir Tristram, with

"Why skip ye so, Sir Fool?"

This half-contemptuous view is very painful to

the Gentle Reader who, though he may seem to some to take his poetry too lightly, is disposed to take his humor rather seriously. Humor seems to him to belong to the higher part of our nature. It is not the enjoyment of a grotesque image in a convex mirror, but, rather, the recognition of fleeting forms of truth.

"I have brought you a funny book, Gentle Reader," says the Professional Humorist.

"Thank you," he answers, struggling against his melancholy forebodings. "You will pardon me if I seem to take my pleasures sadly."

It is hard for him to force a smile as he watches the procession of jokes, each as broad as it is long. This ostentatious jocosity is not to his liking.

"Thackeray," he says, "defines humor as a mixture of love and wit. Humor, therefore, being of the nature of love, should not behave itself unseemly."

He cannot bear to see it obtruding itself upon the public. Its proper habit is to hide from observation "as if the wren taught it concealment." When a Happy Thought ventures abroad it should be as a royal personage traveling *incognito*.

This is a big world, and it is serious business

to live in it.  It makes many demands.  It requires intensity of thought and strenuousness of will and solidity of judgment.  Great tasks are set before us.  We catch fugitive glimpses of beauty, and try to fix them forever in perfect form, — that is the task of art.  We see thousands of disconnected facts, and try to arrange them in orderly sequence, — that is the task of science.  We see the ongoing of eternal force, and seek some reason for it, — that is the task of philosophy.

But when art and science and philosophy have done their best, there is a great deal of valuable material left over.  There are facts that will not fit into any theory, but which keep popping up at us from the most unexpected places.  Nobody can tell where they come from or why they are here ; but here they are.  Try as hard as we may for perfection, the net result of our labors is an amazing variety of imperfectnesses.  We are surprised at our own versatility in being able to fail in so many different ways.  Everything is under the reign of strict law; but many queer things happen, nevertheless.  What are we to do with all the waifs and strays ?  What are we to do with all the sudden incongruities which mock at our wisdom and destroy the symmetry of our ideas?

The solemnly logical intelligence ignores their existence. It does not trouble itself about anything which does not belong to its system. The system itself has such perfect beauty that it is its own excuse for being.

More sensitive and less self-centred natures do not find the way so easy. They allow themselves to be worried by the incongruities which they cannot ignore. It seems to them that whenever they are in earnest the world conspires to mock them. Continually they feel that intellect and conscience are insulted by whipper-snappers of facts that have no right to be in an orderly universe. They can expose a lie, and feel a certain superiority in doing it; but a little unclassified, irreconcilable truth drives them to their wit's end. There it stands in all its shameless actuality asking, "What do you make of me?"

Just here comes the beneficent mission of humor. It takes these unassorted realities that are the despair of the sober intelligence, and extracts from them pure joy. If life depends on the perpetual adjustment of the organism to its environment, humor is the means by which the intellectual life is sustained on those occasions when the expected environment is not there. The adjustment must be made, without a moment's warning, to an altogether new set of conditions. We are called upon to swap horses while crossing the stream. It is a method which the serious minded person does not approve. While arguing the matter he is unhorsed, and finds himself floundering in the water. The humorist accepts the situation instantly. As he scrambles upon his new nag it is with a sense of triumph, for the moment at least, he feels that he has the best of the bargain.

One may have learned to enjoy the sublime, the beautiful, the useful, the orderly, but he has missed something if he has not also learned to enjoy the incongruous, the illusive, and the unexpected. Artistic sensibility finds its satisfaction only in the perfect. Humor is the frank enjoyment of the imperfect. Its objects are not so high, — but there are more of them.

Evolution is a cosmic game of Pussy wants a corner. Each creature has its eye on some snug

corner where it would rest in peace.   Each corner is occupied by some creature that is not
altogether satisfied and that is on the lookout
for a larger sphere.   There is much beckoning
between those who are desirous of making a
change.   Now and then some bold spirit gives
up his assured position and scrambles for something better.   The chances are that the adven-
turer finds it harder to attain the coveted place
than he had thought.   For the fact is that there
are not corners enough to go around.   If there
were enough corners, and every one were content
to stay in the one where he found himself at the
beginning, then the game would be impossible.
It is well that this never happens.   Nature looks
after that.   When things are too homogeneous
she breaks them up into new and amazing kinds
of heterogeneity.   It is a good game, and one
learns to like it after he enters into the spirit
of it.

If the Universe had a place for everything
and everything was in its place, there would be
little demand for humor.   As a matter of fact
the world is full of all sorts of people, and they
are not all in their proper places.   There are

amazing incongruities between station and character. It is not a world that has been reduced
to order; it is still in the making. One may
easily grow misanthropic and pessimistic by
dwelling upon the misfits.

> " As to behold desert a beggar born
> And needy nothing trimmed in jollity.
>
> .    .    .    .    .    .    .    .
>
> And art made tongue-tied by authority,
> And simple truth miscalled simplicity,
> And folly doctor-like, controlling skill,
> And captive good attending captain ill.''

But fortunately these incongruities are not
altogether tragical. There are certain moods
when we rather enjoy seeing "needy nothing
trimmed in jollity." We are pleased when Justice Shallow slaps Sir John Falstaff on the back
and says, "Ha! it was a merry night, Sir John."
We are not irritated beyond endurance because
in this world where so many virtuous people have
a hard time, such trifling fellows as Sir Toby and
Sir Andrew have their cakes and ale. When
folly puts on doctor-like airs it is not always
disagreeable. We would not have Dogberry
put off the watch to give place to some one who
could pass the civil service examination.

The humorist, when asked what he thinks of the actual world, would turn upon his questioner as Touchstone turned upon Corin when he was asked how he liked the shepherd's life : —

"Hast any philosophy in thee, shepherd?" The world is not at all like the descriptions of it, and yet he cannot take a very gloomy view of it. In respect to itself it is a good world, and yet in respect that it is not finished it leaves much to be desired. Yet in respect that it leaves much to be desired, and much to be done by us, it is perhaps better *for us* than if it were finished. In respect that many things happen that are opposed to our views of the eternal fitness of things, it is a perplexing world. Yet in respect that we have a faculty for enjoying the occasional unfitness of things, it is delightful. On the whole, he sums up with Touchstone, "It suits my humor well."

Humor is impossible to the man of one idea. There must be at least two ideas moving in opposite directions, so that there may be a collision. Such an accident does not happen in a mind under economical management that runs only one train of thought a day.

There are many ideas that have a very inse-
cure tenure. They hold their own as squatters.
By and by Science will come along and evict
them, but in the mean time these homely folk
make very pleasant neighbors. All they ask is
that we shall not take them too seriously. That
a thing is not to be taken too seriously does not
imply that it is either unreal or unimportant: —
it only means that it is not to be taken that
way. There is, for example, a pickaninny on a
Southern plantation. The anthropologist mea-
sures his skull and calls it by a long Latin name.
The psychologist carefully records his nervous
reactions. The pedagogical expert makes him
the victim of that form of inquisition known as
" child study." The missionary perplexes himself in vain attempting to get at his soul. Then
there comes along a person of another sort. At
the first look, a genial smile of recognition comes
over the face of this new spectator. He is the
first one who has seen the pickaninny. The one
essential truth about a black, chubby, kinky-
haired pickaninny is that, when he rolls up his
eyes till only the whites are visible, he is irresistibly funny. This is what theologians term

" the substance of doctrine " concerning the pickaninny.

When Charles Lamb slipped on the London
pavement, he found delight in watching the
chimney sweep who stood laughing at his misfortune. " There he stood irremovable, as though
the jest were to last forever, with such a max-
imum of glee and minimum of mischief in his
mirth — for the grin of a genuine sweep hath no
malice in it — that I could have been content, if
the honor of a gentleman might endure it, to
have remained his butt and his mockery till
midnight." There were many middle-aged London citizens who could no more appreciate that
kind of pleasure than a Hottentot could appreciate an oratorio. That is only saying that the
average citizen and the average Hottentot have,
as Wordsworth mildly puts it, " faculties which
they have never used."

The high place that humor holds among our
mental processes is evident when we consider
that it is almost the only one that requires that
we shall be thoroughly awake. In our dreams
we have many æsthetic enjoyments, as vague

splendors pass before us.  At other times there
is an abnormal sensitiveness to the sovereignty,
not to say the despotism of ethics.  We feel
burdened with the weight of unpardonable sins.
We are able also in our sleep to philosophize
after a fashion which is, for the time, quite satisfactory.  At such times we are sure that we
have made important discoveries; if we could
only remember what they were.  A thousand
incongruities pass through our minds, but there
is one thing which we cannot do.  We cannot
recognize that they are incongruous.  Such a
discovery would immediately awaken us.

Tennyson tells how

> "half awake I heard
> The parson taking wide and wider sweeps,
> Now harping on the church commissioners,
> Now hawking at Geology and schism."

It would be possible for the parson and his congregation to keep on with that sort of thing
Sunday after Sunday.  They would discover nothing absurd in the performance, so long as they
were in their usual semi-somnolent condition.

Humor implies mental alertness and power of
discrimination.  It also implies a hospitality

toward all the differences that are recognized. Psychologists speak of the Association of Ideas. It is a pleasant thought, but it is, in reality, difficult to induce Ideas to associate in a neighborly way. In many minds the different groups are divided by conventional lines, and there are aristocratic prejudices separating the classes from the masses. The Working Hypothesis, honest son of toil that he is, does not expect so much as a nod of recognition from the High Moral Principle who walks by in his Sunday clothes. The steady Habit does not associate with the high-bred Sentiment. They do not belong to the same set. Only in the mind of the humorist is there a true democracy. Here everybody knows everybody. Even the priggish Higher Thought is not allowed to enjoy a sense of superiority. Plain Common Sense slaps him on the back, calls him by his first name, and bids him not make a fool of himself.

Of the two ingredients which Thackeray mentions, the first, love, is that which gives body; the addition of wit gives the effervescence. The pleasure of wit lies in its unexpectedness. In humor there is the added pleasure of really liking that which surprises us. It is like meeting an old friend in an unexpected place. " What, you here? " we say. This is the kind of pleasure we get from Dr. Johnson's reply to the lady who asked why he had put a certain definition in his dictionary: " Pure ignorance, madam."

The fact is that long ago we made the acquaintance of one whom Bunyan describes as " a brisk young lad named Ignorance." He is a dear friend of ours, and we are on very familiar terms with him when we are at home; but we do not expect to meet him in fine society. Suddenly we turn the corner, and we see him walking arm in arm with so great a man as Dr. Samuel Johnson. At once we are at our ease in the presence of the great man; it seems we have a mutual acquaintance.

Another element in real humor is a certain detachment of mind. We must not be afraid, or jealous, or angry; in order to take a really humorous view of any character, we must be in a position to see all around it. If I were brought before Fielding's Squire Western on charge of poaching, and if I had a pheasant concealed under my coat, I should not be able to appreciate what an amusing person the squire is. I should be inclined to take him very seriously.

The small boy who pins a paper to the schoolmaster's coat tail imagines that he has achieved a masterpiece of humor. But he is not really in a position to reap the fruits of his perilous adventure. It is a fearful and precarious joy which he feels. What if the schoolmaster should turn around? That would be tragedy. Neither the small boy nor the schoolmaster gets the full flavor of humor. But suppose an old friend of the schoolmaster happens just then to look in at the door. His delight in the situation has a mellowness far removed from the anxious, ambiguous glee of the urchin. He knows that the small boy is not so wicked as he thinks he is, and the schoolmaster is not so terrible as he seems. He remembers the time when the schoolmaster was up to the same pranks. So, from the assured position of middle age, he looks upon the small boy that was and upon the small boy that is, and finds them both very good, — much better, indeed, than at this moment they find each other.

It is this sense of the presence of a tolerant

spectator, looking upon the incidents of the passing hour, which we recognize in the best literature. Books that are meant simply to be funny are very short-lived. The first reception of a joke awakens false expectations. It is received with extravagant heartiness. But when, encouraged by this hospitality, it returns again and again, its welcome is worn out. There is something melancholy in a joke deserted in its old age.

The test of real literature is that it will bear repetition. We read over the same pages again and again, and always with fresh delight. This bars out all mere jocosity. A certain kind of wit, which depends for its force on mere verbal brilliancy, has the same effect. The writers whom we love are those whose humor does not glare or glitter, but which has an iridescent quality. It is the perpetual play of light and color which enchants us. We are conscious all the time that the light is playing on a real thing. It is something more than a clever trick; there is an illumination.

Erasmus, in dedicating his "Praise of Folly" to Sir Thomas More, says: —

"I conceived that this would not be least approved by you, inasmuch as you are wont to be delighted with such kind of pleasantry as is neither unlearned nor altogether insipid. Such is your sweetness of temper that you can and like to carry yourself to all men a man of all hours. Unless an overweening opinion of myself may have made me blind, I have praised folly not altogether foolishly. I have moderated my style, that the understanding reader may perceive that my endeavor is to make mirth rather than to bite."

Erasmus has here described a kind of humor that is consistent with seriousness of purpose. The characteristics he notes are good temper, insight into human nature, a certain reserve, and withal a gentle irony that makes the praise of folly not unpleasing to the wise. It is a way of looking at things characteristic of men like Chaucer and Cervantes and Montaigne and Shakespeare, and Bunyan and Fielding and Addison, Goldsmith, Charles Lamb and Walter Scott. In America, we have seen it in Irving and Dr. Holmes and James Russell Lowell.

I have left out of the list one whom nature

endowed for the supreme man of humor among Englishmen, — Jonathan Swift. Charles Lamb argues against the common notion that it is a misfortune to a man to have a surly disposition. He says it is not his misfortune; it is the misfortune of his neighbors. It is our misfortune that the man who might have been the English Cervantes had a surly disposition. Dean Swift's humor would have been irresistible, if it had only been good humor.

One of the best examples of humor pervading a work of the utmost seriousness of purpose is Bunyan's "Pilgrim's Progress." The "Pilgrim's Progress" is not a funny book; the humor is not tacked on as a moral is tacked on to a fable, nor does it appear by way of an interlude to relieve the tension of the mind. It is so deeply interfused, so a part and parcel of the religious teaching, that many readers overlook it altogether. One may read the book a dozen times without a smile, and after that he may recognize the touch of the born humorist on every page. Bunyan himself recognized the quality of his work : —

"Some there be that say he laughs too loud,
And some do say his head is in a cloud.

.   .   .   .   .   .   .   .   .   .   .

One may, I think, say both his laughs and cries
May well be guessed at by his wat'ry eyes.
Some things are of that nature as to make
One's fancy chuckle, while his heart doth ache."

There speaks the real humorist; not the Merry Andrew laughing at his meaningless pranks, but one whose quick imagination is at play when his conscience is most overtasked. Even in the Valley of Humiliation, where the fierce Apollyon was wont to fright the pilgrims, they heard a boy singing cheerily, —

"He that is down need fear no fall."

And Mr. Great Heart said: "Do you hear him? I dare say that boy lives a merrier life, and wears more of the herb called heart's-ease in his bosom, than he that is clad in silk and velvet." It is a fine spirit that can find time, on such a strenuous pilgrimage, to listen to these wayside songs.

Take the character sketch of Mr. Fearing: —

"Now as they walked together, the guide asked the old gentleman if he did not know one Mr. Fearing that came on a pilgrimage out of his parts?

" *Honest.* Yes, very well, said he.  He was a man that had the root of the matter in him, but he was one of the most troublesome pilgrims that ever I met in all my days.

" *Great Heart.* Why, he was always afraid he should come short of whither he had a desire to go.  Everything frightened him that he heard anybody speak of that had but the least appearance of opposition in it.  I hear that he lay roaring in the Slough of Despond for about a month together. . . . Well, after he had lain in the Slough of Despond a great while, as I have told you, one sunshine morning, I do not know how, he ventured and so got over ; but when he was over he would scarce believe it.  He had, I believe, a Slough of Despond in his mind, a slough he carried everywhere with him. . . . When he came to the Hill Difficulty he made no stick at that ; nor did he much fear the lions; for you must know his trouble was not about such things as those. . . . When he was come at Vanity Fair, I thought he would have fought with all the men at the fair. . . . He was a man of choice spirit though he kept himself very low."

Poor Mr. Fearing.  We all have been made

uncomfortable by him. But we love Bunyan
for that touch about the lions, for we know it
is true. Easy things go hard with Mr. Fearing;
but give him something difficult, like going up
San Juan hill in the face of a withering fire, and
Mr. Fearing can keep up with the best Rough
Rider of them all. It takes Mr. Great Heart to
do justice to Mr. Fearing.

It is the mission of a kindly humor to take a
person full of foibles and weaknesses and suddenly to reveal his unsuspected nobleness. And
there is considerable room for this kind of treatment; for there are a great many lovable people whose virtues are not chronic, but sporadic.
These virtues grow up, one knows not how,
without visible means of support in the general
character, and in defiance of moral science; and
yet it is a real pleasure to see them.

There are two very different kinds of humor.
One we naturally describe as a flavor, the other
as an atmosphere. We speak of the flavor of
the essays of Charles Lamb. It is a discovery
we make very much as Bobo made the discovery
of roast pig. The mind of Charles Lamb was
like a capacious kettle hanging from the crane in

the fireplace; all sorts of savory ingredients were thrown into it, and the whole was kept gently simmering, but never allowed to come to the boil.

Lamb says, " C. declares that a man cannot have a good conscience who refuses apple dumpling, and I confess that I am of the same opinion." I am inclined to pass that kind of judgment on the person who does not have a comfortable feeling of satisfaction in reading for the twentieth time The Complaint on the Decay of Beggars, and the Praise of Chimney Sweepers.

Charles Lamb is not jocose. He likes to theorize. Now, your prosaic theorist has a very laborious task. He tries to get all the facts under one formula. This is very ticklish business. It is like the game of Pigs in Clover. He gets all the facts but one into the inner circle. By a dexterous thrust he gets that one in, and the rest are out.

Lamb is a philosopher who does not have this trouble. He does not try to fit all the facts to one theory. That seems to him too economical, when theories are so cheap. With large-hearted generosity he provides a theory for every fact.

He clothes the ragged exception with all the decent habiliments of a universal law. He picks up a little ragamuffin of a fact, and warms its heart and points out its great relations. He is not afraid of generalizing from insufficient data; he has the art of making a delightful summer out of a single swallow. When we turn to the essay on the Melancholy of Tailors, we do not think of asking for statistics. If one tailor was melancholy, that was enough to justify the generalization. When we find a tailor who is not melancholy, it will be time to make another theory to fit his case.

This is the charm of Lamb's letter to the gentleman who inquired " whether a person at the age of sixty-three, with no more proficiency than a tolerable knowledge of most of the characters of the English alphabet amounts to, by dint of persevering application and good masters, may hope to arrive within a presumable number of years at that degree of attainment that would entitle the possessor to the character of a *learned man*." The answer is candid, serious, and exhaustive. No false hopes are encouraged. The difficulties are plainly set forth. " However," it is said, "where all cannot be compassed, much may be accomplished; but I must not, in fairness, conceal from you that you have much to do." The question is thoroughly discussed as to whether it would be well for him to enter a primary school. "You say that you stand in need of emulation; that this incitement is nowhere to be had but in the public school. But have you considered the nature of the emulation belonging to those of tender years which you would come in competition with?"

Do you think these dissertations a waste of time? If you do, it is sufficient evidence that you sadly need them; for they are the antitoxin to counteract the bacillus of pedantry. Were I appointed by the school board to consider the applicants for teachers' certificates, after they had passed the examination in the arts and sciences, I should subject them to a more rigid test. I should hand each candidate Lamb's essays on The Old and New Schoolmaster and on Imperfect Sympathies. I should make him read them to himself, while I sat by and watched. If his countenance never relaxed, as if he were inwardly saying, "That's so," I should withhold the certificate.  I should not consider him a fit person to have charge of innocent youth.

Just as we naturally speak of the flavor of Charles Lamb, so we speak of the atmosphere of Cervantes or of Fielding.  We are out of doors in the sunshine.  All sorts of people are doing all sorts of things in all sorts of ways; and we are glad that we are there to see them. It is one of the

> " charmèd days
> When the Genius of God doth flow;
> The wind may alter twenty ways
> But a tempest cannot blow."

On such days it does n't matter what happens. We are not "under the weather," but consciously superior to it.  We are in no mood to grumble over mishaps, — the more the merrier. The master of the revels has made the brave announcement that his programme shall be carried out " rain or shine," and henceforth we have no anxieties.

This diffused good-humor can only come from a mind which is free from any taint of morbidness.  It is that merry-heartedness that " doth good like medicine."  It is an overflowing friendliness, which brings a laughter that is without scorn.

This kind of humor is possible only among persons who are thoroughly congenial, and who take mutual good-will for granted. It is for this reason that it is so difficult to translate it or to carry it from one community to another. It is customary for every nation to bring the accusation against foreigners that they are destitute of the sense of humor. Even peoples so near akin as the English and Americans cherish such suspicions. The American is likely to feel that his English friends do not receive his pleasantries with that punctuality which is the politeness of kings. They are conscientious enough and eventually do the right thing; but procrastination is the thief of wit as well as of time. But we, on our side, are equally slow, and Mr. Punch often causes anxious thoughts.

The real difficulty is not in understanding what is said but in appreciating that which should be taken for granted. The stranger does not see the serious background of sober thought and genuine admiration, into which the amusing figures suddenly intrude. The frontiersman

would see no point in a story that might delight
a common room in Oxford.   What if a bishop
did act in an undignified manner or commit a
blunder?  Why should n't he — like the rest of
us?  To enjoy his foibles one must first have a
realizing sense of what a great man a bishop is,
and how surprising it is that, now and then, he
should step down from his pedestal.

On the other hand, the real humor of the
frontier is missed by one who has not learned to
take seriously the frontiersman's life and who
has not entered into his habitual point of view.

Dickens is an example of the way in which a
man's humor is limited to the sphere of his sympathies.   How genial is the atmosphere which
surrounds Mr. Pickwick and Mr. Sam Weller!
Whatever they do, they can never go wrong.
But when we turn to the "American Notes" or to
the American part of " Martin Chuzzlewit," we
are conscious of a difference.  There is no atmosphere to relieve the dreariness.   Mr. Jefferson
Brick is not amusing ; he is odious.   The people
on the Ohio River steamer do not make us smile
by their absurdities.   Dickens lets us see how he
despises them all.   He is fretful and peevish.

He fails utterly to catch the humor of the frontier. He is unable to follow out the hint which Mark Tapley gave when, looking over the dreary waste of Eden on the Mississippi, he said apologetically, " Eden ain't all built yet."

To an Englishman that does not mean much, but to an American it is wonderfully appealing. Martin Chuzzlewit saw only the ignominious contrast between the prospectus and the present reality. Eden was a vulgar fraud, and that was the whole of it. The American, with invincible optimism, looking upon the same scene, sees something more ! He smiles, perhaps, a little cynically at the incongruity between the prospectus and the present development, and then his fancy chuckles at what his fancy sees in the future. " Eden ain't all built yet," — that 's a fact. But just think what Eden will be when it is all built !

By the way, there is one particularly good thing about the atmosphere ; it prevents our being hit by meteors. The meteor, when it strikes the upper air, usually ignites, and that is the end of it. There are some minds that

have not enough atmosphere to protect them.
They are pelted continually; whatever is unpleasant comes to them in solid chunks. There
are others more fortunately surrounded, who
escape this impact. All that is seen is a flash
in the upper air. They are none the worse for
passing through a meteoric shower of petty mis-
fortunes.

The mind that is surrounded by an atmosphere of humorous suggestiveness is also favored
in its outlook upon the shortcomings of mankind.
Their angularities are softened and become less
uniformly unpleasing. That fine old English
divine, Dr. South, has a sermon in which he
defends the thesis that it is a greater guilt to
enjoy the contemplation of our neighbor's sins
than to commit the same offences in our proper
persons. That seems to me to be very hard
doctrine. I am inclined to make a distinction.
There are some faults which ought to be taken
seriously at all times, but there are others which
the neighbors should be allowed to enjoy, if they
can.

Indeed, it is the genuine reformer who is seek-
ing to right great wrongs who most needs the

capacity to distinguish between grave evils and peccadillos. A measure of good-humored tolerance for human weakness is a part of his equipment for effective work. Lacking in this, he is doomed to perpetual irritation and disappointment. He mistakes friends for foes and wages a losing battle. He is likely to be the victim of a moral egoism which distorts the facts of experience and confuses his personal whims with his disinterested purposes. His great ideal is lost sight of in some petty strife. Above all, he loses the power of endurance in the time of partial failure.

The contest of wits between the inventors of projectiles and the makers of armor plate seemed at one time settled by Harvey's process for rendering the surface of the resisting steel so hard that the missiles hurled against it were shattered. The answer of the gun-makers was made by attaching a tip of softer metal to the shell. The soft tip received the first shock of the impact, and it was found that the penetrating power of the shell was increased enormously. The scientific explanation I have forgotten. I may, however, hazard an anthropomorphic explanation.

If there is any human nature in the atoms of
steel, I can see a great advantage in having the
softer particles go before the hard, to have a
momentary yielding before the inevitable crash.
When they are hurtling through the air, tense
and strained by the initial velocity till it seems
that they must fly apart, it is a great thing to
have a group of good-humored, happy-go-lucky
atoms in the front, who call out cheerily: "Come
along, boys! Don't take it too hard; we 're in
for it." And sure enough, before they have
time to fall apart they are in. Those whose
thoughts and purposes have most penetrated the
hard prejudices of their time have learned this
lesson.

Your unhumorous reformer, with painful intensity of moral self-consciousness, cries out: —

"The time is out of joint: O cursed spite,
That ever I was born to set it right!"

He takes himself and his cause always with equal
seriousness. He hurls himself against the accumulated wrongs and the invincible ignorance
of the world, and there is a great crash; but
somehow, the world seems to survive the shock
better than he does. It is a tough old world,

and bears a great deal of pounding. Indeed, it
has been pounded so much and so long that it
has become quite solid.

Now and then, however, there comes along a
reformer whose zeal is tipped with humor. His
thought penetrates where another man's is only
shattered. That is what made Luther so effective. He struck heavy blows at the idols men
adored. But he was such a genial, whole-souled
iconoclast that those who were most shocked at
him could not help liking him — between times.
He would give a smashing blow at the idol, and
then a warm hand grasp and a hearty "God
bless you" to the idolater; and then idolater
and iconoclast would be down on the floor together, trying to see if there were any pieces of
the idol worth saving. It was all so unexpected
and so incongruous and so shocking, and yet so
unaffectedly religious and so surprisingly the
right thing to do, that the upshot of it all was
that people went away saying, "Dr. Martin is n't
such a bad fellow, after all."

Luther's "Table Talk" penetrated circles which
were well protected against his theological treatises. Men were conscious of a good humor even

in his invective ; for he usually gave them time
to see the kindly twinkle in his eye before he
knocked them down.

In order to engage Karlstadt in a controversy,
Luther drew out a florin from his pocket and
cried heartily, " Take it ! Attack me boldly ! "
Karlstadt took it, put it in his purse, and gave
it to Luther. Luther then drank to his health.
Then Karlstadt pledged Luther. Then Luther
said, " The more violent your attacks, the more
I shall be delighted." Then they gave each
other their hands and parted. One can almost
be reconciled to theological controversy, when it
is conducted in a manner so truly sportsmanlike.

Luther had a way of characterizing a person
in a sentence, that was much more effective than
his labored vituperation (in which, it must be
confessed, he was a master). Thus, speaking of
the attitude of Erasmus, he said, " Erasmus
stands looking at creation like a calf at a new
door." It was very unjust to Erasmus, and yet
the picture sticks in the mind ; for it is such a
perfect characterization of the kind of mind that
we are all acquainted with, which looks at the
marvels of creation with the wide-eyed gaze of

bovine youthfulness, curious, not to know how
that door came there, but only to know whether
it leads to something to eat.

The humor of Luther suggests that of Abraham Lincoln. Both were men of the people, and
their humor had a flavor of the soil. They were
alike capable of deep dejection, but each found
relief in spontaneous laughter. The surprise of
the grave statesman when Lincoln would preface
a discussion with a homely anecdote of the frontier was of the same kind felt by the sixteenth-
century theologians when Luther turned aside
from his great arguments, which startled Europe,
to tell a merry tale in ridicule of the pretensions
of the monks.

If I were to speak of the humorist as a philosopher, some of the gravest of the philosophers
would at once protest. Humor, they say, has no
place in their philosophy; and they are quite
right. Indeed, it is doubtful if a humorist would
ever make a good, systematic philosopher. He
is a modest person. He is only a gleaner following the reapers; but he manages to pick up
a great many grains of wisdom which they overlook.

Dante pictures the sages of antiquity as forever walking on a verdant mead, "with eyes slow and grave, and with great authority in their looks;" as if, in the other world, they were continually oppressed by the wisdom they had acquired in this. But I can imagine a gathering of philosophers in a different fashion. Gravely they have come, each bearing his ponderous volume, in which he has explained the universe and settled the destiny of mankind. Then, suddenly, in contrast with their theories, the reality is disclosed. The incorrigible pedants and dogmatists turn away in sullen disappointment; but from all true lovers of wisdom there arises a peal of mellow laughter, as each one realizes the enormous incongruity between what he knew and what he thought he knew.

The discovery that things are not always as they seem is one that some people make in this world. They get a glimpse of something that is going on behind the scenes, and their smile is very disconcerting to the sober spectators around them.

Sometimes it is the bitter smile of disillusion. Matthew Arnold wrote of Heine : —

> " The Spirit of the world,
>    Beholding the absurdity of men, —
>    Their vaunts, their feats, — let a sardonic smile,
>    For one short moment, wander o'er his lips.
>    That smile was Heine."

But there is another kind of smile evoked by the incongruity between the appearance and the reality. It is the smile that comes when behind some mask that had affrighted us we recognize a familiar and friendly face. There is a smile which is not one of disillusion. There is a philosophy which is dissolved in humor. The wise man sees the incongruities involved in the very nature of things. They are the result of the free play of various forces. To his quick insight the actual world is no more like the formal descriptions of it than the successive attitudes of a galloping horse are like the pose of an equestrian statue. His mind catches instantaneous views of this world as its elements are continually dissolving and re-combining. It is all very surprising, and he smiles as he sees how much better they turn out than might be expected.

> " Sad-eyed Fakirs swiftly say
>    Endless dirges to decay.
>
>    ·    ·    ·    ·    ·    ·

And yet it seemeth not to me
That the high gods love tragedy;
For Saadi sat in the sun.

.    .    .    .    .    .    .

Sunshine in his heart transferred,
Lighted each transparent word.

.    .    .    .    .    .    .

And thus to Saadi said the Muse:
' Eat thou the bread which men refuse;
Flee from the goods which from thee flee;
Seek nothing, — Fortune seeketh thee.

.    .    .    .    .    .    .

On thine orchard's edge belong
All the brags of plume and song.

.    .    .    .    .    .    .

Nor scour the seas, nor sift mankind,
A poet or a friend to find:
Behold, he watches at the door!
Behold his shadow on the floor! ' "

In the book of Proverbs, Wisdom says, " I,
Wisdom, dwell with Prudence." But there is
another member of the household. It is Humor,
sister of serene Wisdom and of the heavenly
Prudence. She does not often laugh, and when
she does it is mostly at her sister Wisdom, who
cannot long resist the infection. There is not
one set smile upon her face, as if she contemplated
an altogether amusing world. The smiles that

come and go are shy, elusive things, but they cannot remain long in hiding.

Wisdom, from her high house, takes wide views, and Prudence peers anxiously into the future; but gentle Humor loves to take short views; she delights in homely things, and continually finds surprises in that which is most familiar. Wisdom goes on laborious journeys, and comes home bringing her treasures from afar; and Humor matches them, every one, with what she has found in the dooryard.

# Cases of Conscience
# Concerning Witchcrafts

-----

THAT was a curious state of things in Salem village. There was the Meeting-House in plain sight, with sermons every Sunday and lectures on week-days. There were gospel privileges for all, and the path of duty was evident enough for the simplest understanding. Nevertheless, certain persons who should have listened to the sermons, when they heard the sound of a trumpet hied to the rendezvous of witches. When haled before the court their only answer was that they could n't help it.

The ministers were disturbed, but being thorough-going men, they did not rest content with academic discussion of the question of the falling-off in church attendance. They inquired into its cause, and became convinced that they were dealing with sorcery.  All this is duly set down in Increase Mather's treatise on " Cases of Conscience concerning Witchcrafts."

This method of inquisition is commended to those writers who look upon the Gentle Reader's love of Romance as a deadly sin.  The trouble, as I understand it, is this.  A number of gentlemen devoted to literature have cultivated style till it is as near a state of utter perfection as human nature will tolerate.  Indeed, they emulate that classic writer of whom Roger Ascham remarked that he labored " with uncontented care to write better than he could."  They have attained such accuracy of observation and such skill in the choice of words that the man in the book is as like to the man on the street as two peas.  They are also skilled in criticism and are able to prove that it is our duty not only to admire but also to read their books.  The complaint is that the readers, instead of walking in the path of duty, troop off after some mere story-teller who has never passed an examination in Pathology, and who is utterly incapable of making an exhaustive analysis of motives.

The Gentle Reader when he hears the accusations of the stern realists makes no denial of the facts. He admits that he likes a good story better than an involved study of character. He listens to the reproofs with the helplessness of one who has only the frail barrier of a personal taste to shield him from the direct blow of the categorical imperative. If personal taste were to be accepted as a sufficient plea, he is aware that the most besotted inebriate would go unwhipped of justice. In this predicament he shields himself behind his favorite authors. If there be a fault it is theirs, not his. They have bewitched him by their spells. It is impossible for him to withstand the potent enchantments of these wizards.

I am inclined to think that there is much justice in this view of the matter and that the militant realists should turn their attention from the innocent reader to those who have power to bewitch him.

The accepted signs of witchcraft, as enumerated by the Mathers, are present. Thus we are told: "A famous Divine recites among other Convictions of a Witch, the Testimony of

the Party bewitched, together with the joint
Oaths of sufficient Persons that they have seen
Prodigious Pranks or Feats wrought by the
Party accused."

This was the kind of evidence relied upon in
the case of G. B. in the Court of Oyer and Ter-
miner held at Salem in 1692. " He was accused by
Nine Persons for extraordinary Lifting and such
Feats of Strength as could not be done without
Diabolical Assistance." It was said that "though
he was a Puny Man yet he had done things beyond the strength of a Giant. A Gun of about
seven foot Barrel, and so heavy that strong Men
could not steadily hold it out with both hands ;
there were several Testimonies that he made nothing of taking up such a Gun behind the Lock,
with one hand, and holding it out like a Pistol
at arm's end." Any readers of romance can tell
of many such prodigious pranks which, while the
spell was upon them, seemed altogether credible.

The test which was looked upon as infallible
by those judicious judges who put little confidence in the flotation of witches on the mill
pond, was that of the lack of intellectual con-
sistency. " Faltering, faulty, inconstant, and

contrary answers upon judicial and deliberate Examination are accounted unlucky symptoms of guilt."

Such inconsistencies may be found in all romantic fiction; yet the magicians seem to have the power to make all things appear probable. I might tell what a pleasant thrill is sometimes produced by these sorceries, but I had better follow the policy of Cotton Mather, who declined to tell all he knew about the Invisible World, lest he might make witchcraft too attractive. " I will not speak plainly lest I should, unaware, poison some of my Readers, as the pious Hermingius did one of his Pupils when he only by way of Diversion recited a Spell."

Cotton Mather makes a suggestion which is of value in regard to the different grades of witches and other wonder-working spirits. His remarks upon this head are so judicious that they should be quoted in full.

"Thirdly, 't is to be supposed, that some *Devils* are more peculiarly *Commission'd*, and perhaps *Qualify'd*, for some Countries, while others are for others. This is intimated when in *Mar.* 5. 10. The Devils *besought* our Lord much, *that he would not send them away out of the Countrey*. Why was that? But in all probability, because *these Devils* were more able to *do the works of the Devil*, in such a Countrey, than in another. It is not likely that every Devil does know every *Language;* or that every Devil can do every *Mischief*. 'T is possible, that the *Experience*, or, if I may call it so, the *Education* of all Devils is not alike, and that there may be some difference in their *Abilities*. If one might make an Inference from what the Devils *do*, to what they *are*, One cannot forbear dreaming, that there are *degrees* of Devils. Who can allow, that such Trifling *Demons*, as that of *Mascon*, or those that once infested our New-berry, are of so much Grandeur, as those *Demons*, whose Games are mighty Kingdoms? Yea, 't is certain, that all Devils do not make a like figure in the *Invisible World*. Nor does it look agreeably, That the *Demons*, which were Familiars of such a Man as the old *Apollonius*, differ not from those baser Goblins that chuse to Nest in the filthy and loathsome Rags of a beastly Sorceress. Accordingly, why may not some Devils be more accomplished for what is to be done in such and such places, when others must be *detach'd* for other Territories? Each Devil, as he sees his advantage, cries out, *Let me be in this Countrey, rather than another.*"

It is only on the theory of bewitchment by a trifling demon who belongs to the lower orders of the literary world that I can account for the sad fall of the reader whose confession follows. Carefully shielded in his youth from all the enticements of the imagination, he yet fell from grace. The unfortunate person seems to be lacking in strength of will, and yet to have some good in him. In my opinion he was more sinned against than sinning. But I will let him tell his story in his own way.

### A CONFESSION

One half the world does not know what the other half reads; but good people are now taught that the first requisite of sociological virtue is to interest themselves in the other half. I therefore venture to call attention to a book that has pleased me, though my delight in it may at once class me with the " submerged tenth " of the reading public. It is "The Pirate's Own Book."

By way of preface to a discussion of this volume, let me make a personal explanation of the causes which led me to its perusal. My reading of such a book cannot be traced to early habit. In my boyhood I had no opportunity to study the careers of pirates, for I was confined to another variety of literature. On Sunday afternoons I read aloud a book called " The Afflicted Man's Companion." The unfortunate gentleman portrayed in this work had a large assortment of afflictions, — if I remember rightly, one for each day of the month, — but among them was nothing so exciting as being marooned in the South Seas. Indeed, his afflictions were of a generalized and abstract kind, which he could have borne with great cheerfulness had it not been for the consolations which were remorselessly administered to him.

If I have become addicted to tales of piracy, I must attribute it to the literary criticisms of too strenuous realists. Before I read them, I took an innocent pleasure in romantic fiction. Without any compunction of conscience I rejoiced in Walter Scott; and when he failed I was pleased even with his imitators. My heart leaped up when I beheld a solitary horseman on the first page, and I did not forsake the horseman, even though I knew he was to be personally conducted through his journey by Mr. G. P. R. James. Fenimore Cooper, in those days, before I was awakened to the nature of literary sin, I found altogether pleasant. The cares of the world faded away, and a soothing conviction of the essential rightness of things came over me, as the pioneers and Indians discussed in deliberate fashion the deepest questions of the universe, between shots. As for stories of the sea, I never thought of being critical. I was ready to take thankfully anything with a salty flavor, from "Sindbad the Sailor" to Mr. Clark Russell. I had no inconvenient knowledge to interfere with my enjoyment. All nautical language was alike impressive, and all nautical manœuvres were to me alike perilous. It would have been a poor Ancient Mariner who could not have enthralled me, when

> "He held me with his skinny hand;
> 'There was a ship,' quoth he."

And if the ship had raking masts and no satisfactory clearance papers, that was enough; as to what should happen, I left that altogether to the author. That the laws of probability held on the Spanish Main as on dry land, I never dreamed.

But after being awakened to the sin of romance, I saw that to read a novel merely for recreation is not permissible. The reader must be put upon oath, and before he allows himself to enjoy any incident must swear that everything is exactly true to life as he has seen it. All vagabonds and sturdy vagrants who have no visible means of support, in the present order of things, are to be driven out of the realm of well-regulated fiction. Among these are included all knights in armor; all rightful heirs with a strawberry mark; all horsemen, solitary or otherwise; all princes in disguise; all persons who are in the habit of saying "prithee," or "Odzooks," or "by my halidome;" all fair ladies who have no irregularities of feature and no realistic incoherencies of speech; all lovers who fall in love at first sight, and who are married at the end of the book and live happily ever after; all witches, fortune-tellers, and gypsies; all spotless heroes and deep-dyed villains; all pirates, buccaneers,

North American Indians with a taste for metaphysics ; all scouts, hunters, trappers, and other individuals who do not wear store clothes. According to this decree, all readers are forbidden to aid and abet these persons, or to give them shelter in their imagination. A reader who should incite a writer of fiction to romance would be held as an accessory before the fact.

After duly repenting of my sins and renouncing my old acquaintances, I felt a preëminent virtue. Had I met the Three Guardsmen, one at a time or all together, I should have passed them by without stopping for a moment's converse. I should have recognized them for the impudent Gascons that they were, and should have known that there was not a word of truth in all their adventures. As for Stevenson's fine old pirate, with his contemptible song about a "dead men's chest and a bottle of rum," I should not have tolerated him for an instant. Instead, I should have turned eagerly to some neutral-tinted person who never had any adventure greater than missing the train to Dedham, and I should have analyzed his character, and agitated myself in the attempt to get at his feelings, and I should have verified

his story by a careful reference to the railway
guide. I should have treated that neutral-tinted
character as a problem, and I should have noted
all the delicate shades in the futility of his conduct. When, on any occasion that called for
action, he did not know his own mind, I should
have admired him for his resemblance to so many
of my acquaintances who do not know their own
minds. After studying the problem until I came
to the last chapter, I should suddenly have given
it up, and agreed with the writer that it had no
solution. In my self-righteousness, I despised
the old-fashioned reader who had been lured on
in the expectation that at the last moment something thrilling might happen.

But temptations come at the unguarded point.
I had hardened myself against romance in fiction,
but I had not been sufficiently warned against
romance in the guise of fact. When in a book-
stall I came upon " The Pirate's Own Book," it
seemed to answer a felt want. Here at least,
outside the boundaries of strict fiction, I could be
sure of finding adventure, and feel again with .
Sancho Panza " how pleasant it is to go about in
expectation of accidents."

I am well aware that good literature — to use Matthew Arnold's phrase — is a criticism of life. But the criticism of life, with its discriminations between things which look very much alike, is pretty serious business. We cannot keep on criticising life without getting tired after a while, and longing for something a little simpler. There is a much-admired passage in Ferishtah's Fancies, in which, after mixing up the beans in his hands and speculating on their color, Ferishtah is not able to tell black from white. Ferishtah, living in a soothing climate, could stand an indefinite amount of this sort of thing; and, moreover, we must remember that he was a dervish, and dervishry, although a steady occupation, is not exacting in its requirements. In our more stimulating climate, we should bring on nervous prostration if we gave ourselves unremittingly to the discrimination between all the possible variations of blackishness and whitishness. We must relieve our minds by occasionally finding something about which there can be no doubt. When my eyes rested on the woodcut that adorns the first page of "The Pirate's Own Book," I felt the rest that comes from perfect certainty in my own moral judgment. Ferishtah himself could not have mixed me up. Here was black without a redeeming spot. On looking upon this pirate, I felt relieved from any criticism of life; here was something beneath criticism. I was no longer tossed about on a chop sea, with its conflicting waves of feeling and judgment, but was borne along triumphantly on a bounding billow of moral reprobation.

As I looked over the headings of the chapters, I was struck by their straightforward and undisguised character. When I read the chapter entitled The Savage Appearance of the Pirates, and compared this with the illustrations, I said, " How true! " Then there was a chapter on the Deceitful Character of the Malays. I had always suspected that the Malays were deceitful, and here I found my impressions justified by competent authority. Then I dipped into the preface, and found the same transparent candor. " A piratical crew," says the author, " is generally formed of the desperadoes and renegades of every clime and nation." Again I said, " Just what I should have expected. The writer is evidently one who 'nothing extenuates.' " Then follows a further description of the pirate : " The pirate, from the perilous nature of his occupation, when not cruising on the ocean, that great highway of nations, selects the most lonely isles of the sea for his retreat, or secretes himself near the shores of bays and lagoons of thickly wooded and uninhabited countries." Just the places where I should have expected him to settle.

" The pirate, when not engaged in robbing, passes his time in singing old songs with choruses like, —

> ' Drain, drain the bowl, each fearless soul !
> Let the world wag as it will ;
> Let the heavens growl, let the devil howl,
> Drain, drain the deep bowl and fill ! '

Thus his hours of relaxation are passed in wild and extravagant frolics, amongst the lofty forests and spicy groves of the torrid zone, and amidst the aromatic and beautiful flowering vegetable products of that region."

Again : " With the name of pirate is also associated ideas of rich plunder, — caskets of buried jewels, chests of gold ingots, bags of outlandish coins, secreted in lonely out-of-the-way places, or buried about the wild shores of rivers and unexplored seacoasts, near rocks and trees bearing mysterious marks, indicating where the treasure is hid." "As it is his invariable practice to secrete and bury his booty, and from the perilous life he lives being often killed, he can never revisit the spot again, immense sums remaining buried in these places are irrevocably lost." Is it any wonder that, with such an introduction, I became interested?

After a perusal of the book, I am inclined to think that a pirate may be a better person to read about than some persons who stand higher in the moral scale. Compare, if you will, a pirate and a pessimist. As a citizen and neighbor I should prefer the pessimist. A pessimist is an excellent and highly educated gentleman, who has been so unfortunate as to be born into a world which is inadequate to his expectations. Naturally he feels that he has a grievance, and in airing his grievance he makes himself unpopular; but it is certainly not his fault that the universe is no better than it is. On the other hand, a pirate is a bad character; yet as a subject of biography he is more inspiring than the pessimist. In one case, we have the impression of one

good man in a totally depraved world ; in the
other case, we have a totally depraved man in
what but for him would be a very good world.
I know of nothing that gives one a more genial
appreciation of average human nature, or a
greater tolerance for the foibles of one's acquaintances, than the contrast with an unmitigated pirate.

My copy of " The Pirate's Own Book " belongs
to the edition of 1837.   On the fly-leaf it bore in
prim handwriting the name of a lady who for
many years must have treasured it.   I like to
think of this unknown lady in connection with
the book.   I know that she must have been an
excellent soul, and I have no doubt that her New
England conscience pointed to the moral law as
the needle to the pole ; but she was a wise woman,
and knew that if she was to keep her conscience
in good repair she must give it some reasonable
relaxation.   I am sure that she was a woman of
versatile philanthropy, and that every moment
she had the ability to make two duties grow
where only one had grown before.   After, however, attending the requisite number of lectures
to improve her mind, and considering in com-

mittees plans to improve other people's minds forcibly, and going to meetings to lament over the condition of those who had no minds to improve, this good lady would feel that she had earned a right to a few minutes' respite. So she would take up "The Pirate's Own Book," and feel a creepy sensation that would be an effectual counter-irritant to all her anxieties for the welfare of the race. Things might be going slowly, and there were not half as many societies as there ought to be, and the world might be in a bad way; but then it was not so bad as it was in the days of Black Beard; and the poor people who did not have any societies to belong to were, after all, not so badly off as the sailors whom the atrocious Nicola left on a desert island, with nothing but a blunderbuss and Mr. Brooks's Family Prayer Book. In fact, it is expressly stated that the pirates refused to give them a cake of soap. To be on a desert island destitute of soap made the common evils of life appear trifling. She had been worried about the wicked people who would not do their duty, however faithfully they had been prodded up to it, who would not be life members on payment of fifty dollars, and w'

would not be annual members on payment of a
dollar and signing the constitution, and who in
their hard and impenitent hearts would not even
sit on the platform at the annual meeting ; but
somehow their guilt seemed less extreme after
she had studied again the picture of Captain
Kidd burying his Bible in the sands near Plymouth. A man who would bury his Bible, using a
spade several times too large for him, and who
would strike such a world-defying attitude while
doing it, made the sin of not joining the society
appear almost venial. In this manner she gained
a certain moral perspective ; even after days
when the public was unusually dilatory about
reforms, and the wheels of progress had begun
to squeak, she would get a good night's sleep.
Contrasting the public with the black background of absolute piracy, she grew tolerant of
its shortcomings, and learned the truth of George
Herbert's saying, that "pleasantness of disposition is a great key to do good."

Not only is a pirate a more comfortable person
to read about than a pessimist, but in many re-
spects he is a more comfortable person to read
about than a philanthropist. The minute the

philanthropist is introduced, the author begins to
show his own cleverness by discovering flaws in
his motives.  You begin to see that the poor man
has his limitations.  Perhaps his philanthropies
are of a different kind from yours, and that irritates you.  Musical people, whom I have heard
criticise other musical people, seem more offended
when some one flats just a little than when he
makes a big ear-splitting discord; and moralists
are apt to have the same fastidiousness.  The
philanthropist is made the victim of the most
cruel kind of vivisection, — a character-study.

Here is a fragment of conversation from a
study of character: " 'That was really heroic,'
said Felix.  'That was what he wanted to do,'
Gertrude went on.  'He wanted to be magnanimous; he wanted to have a fine moral pleasure;
he made up his mind to do his duty; he felt
sublime, — that 's how he likes to feel.' "

This leaves the mind in a painful state of suspense.  The first instinct of the unsophisticated
reader is that if the person has done a good deed,
we ought not to begrudge him a little innocent
pleasure in it.  If he is magnanimous, why not
let him feel magnanimous?  But after Gertrude

has made these subtle suggestions we begin to experience something like antipathy for a man who is capable of having a fine moral pleasure; who not only does his duty, but really likes to do it. There is something wrong about him, and it is all the more aggravating because we are not sure just what it is. There is no trouble of that kind in reading about pirates. You cannot make a character-study out of a pirate, — he has no character. You know just where to place him. You do not expect anything good of him, and when you find a sporadic virtue you are correspondingly elated.

For example, I am pleased to read of the pirate Gibbs that he was "affable and communicative, and when he smiled he exhibited a mild and gentle countenance. His conversation was concise and pertinent, and his style of illustration quite original." If Gibbs had been a philanthropist, it is doubtful whether these social and literary graces would have been so highly appreciated.

So our author feels a righteous glow when speaking of the natives of the Malabar coasts, and accounting for their truthfulness: "For as they had been used to deal with pirates, they always found them men of honor in the way of trade, — a people enemies of deceit, and that scorned to rob but in their own way."

He is a very literal-minded person, and takes all his pirates seriously, but often we are surprised by some touch of nature that makes the whole world kin. There was the ferocious Benevedes, who flourished on the west coast of South America, and who, not content with sea power, attempted to gather an army. It is said that " a more finished picture of a pirate cannot be conceived," and the description that follows certainly bears out this assertion. Yet he had his own ideas of civilization, and a power of adaptation that reminds us of the excellent and ingenious Swiss Family Robinson. When he captures the American whaling-ship Hercalia, we are prepared for a wild scene of carnage ; but instead we are told that Benevedes immediately dismantled the ship, and " out of the sails made trousers for half his army." After the trousers had been distributed, Benevedes remarked that his army was complete except in one essential particular, — he had no trumpets for the cavalry : whereupon, at the suggestion of the New Bedford skipper, he ripped off the copper sheets of the vessel, out of which a great variety of copper trumpets were quickly manufactured, and soon "the whole camp resounded with the warlike blasts." While the delighted pirates were enjoying their instrumental music, the skipper and nine of the crew took occasion to escape in a boat which had been imprudently concealed on the river bank.

In the "Proverbial Philosophy" we are told that

"Many virtues weighted by excess sink among the vices,
Many vices, amicably buoyed, float among the virtues."

Had Mr. Tupper been acquainted with the career of Captain Davis of the Spanish Main, he would have found many apt illustrations of his thesis. Captain Davis had the vices incidental to a piratical career, but they were amicably buoyed up by some virtues which would have adorned a different station in life. He was a great stickler for parliamentary law, and everything under his direction was done decently and in order. Whenever it was possible, he made his demands in writing, a method which was businesslike and left no room for misunderstanding.

After a sloop had been seized and duly pillaged, we are informed that : —

"In full possession of the vessel and stores and goods, a large bowl of punch was made. Under its exhilarating influence it was proposed to choose a commander, and to form a future mode of policy. The election was soon over and a large majority of legal voters were in favor of Davis, and, no scrutiny being demanded, Davis was declared duly elected. He then addressed them in a short and appropriate speech."

The chief virtue of Davis seemed to be neatness, which on one occasion he used to admirable advantage. "Encountering a French ship of twenty-four guns, Davis proposed to the crew to attack her, assuring them that she would prove a rich prize. This appeared to the crew such a hazardous enterprise that they were adverse to the measure; but he acquainted them that he had conceived a stratagem that he was confident would succeed."

This stratagem was worthy of the Beau Brummel of pirates. At the critical moment, the crew "according to the direction of Davis appeared on deck in white shirts, which making an ap-

pearance of numbers the Frenchman was intimi-
dated and struck." Why the white shirts should
have given the appearance of numbers it is difficult to understand, but we can well understand
the surprise of the Frenchman over the pirate's
immaculate attire.

Most of the pirates seem to have conducted
their lives on a highly romantic, not to say sen-
sational plan. This reprehensible practice, of
course, must shut them off from the sympathy of
all realists of the stricter school, who hold that
there should be no dramatic situations, and that
even when a story is well begun it should not be
brought to a finish, but should " peter out " in
the last chapters, no one knows how or why.
Sometimes, however, a pirate manages to come
to an end sufficiently commonplace to make a
plot for a most irreproachable novel. There was
Captain Avery. He commenced the practice of
his profession very auspiciously by running away
with a ship of thirty guns from Bristol. In the
Indian Ocean he captured a treasure-ship of the
Great Mogul. In this ship, it is said, "there
were several of the greatest persons of the court."
There was also on board the daughter of the

Great Mogul, who was on a pilgrimage to Mecca.
The painstaking historian comments on this very
justly : " It is well known that the people of the
East travel with great magnificence, so that they
had along with them all their slaves, with a large
quantity of vessels of gold and silver and immense sums of money.  The spoil, therefore, that
Avery received from that ship was almost incal-
culable."  To capture the treasure-ship of the
Great Mogul under such circumstances would
have turned the head of any ordinary pirate who
had weakened his mind by reading works tinged
with romanticism.  His companions, when the
treasure was on board, wished to sail to Mada-
gascar, and there build a small fort; but "Avery
disconcerted the plan and rendered it altogether
unnecessary."  We know perfectly well what
these wretches would have done if they had
been allowed to have their own way. they would
have gathered in one of the spicy groves, and
would have taken up vociferously their song, —

> " Drain, drain the bowl, each fearless soul !
> Let the world wag as it will."

Avery would have none of this, so when most of
the men were away from the ship he sailed off

with the treasure, leaving them to their evil ways, and to a salutary poverty. Here begins the realism of the story. With the treasures of the Great Mogul in his hold, he did not follow the illusive course of Captain Kidd, "as he sailed, as he sailed." He did not even lay his course for the "coasts of Coromandel." Instead of that he made a bee-line for America, with the laudable intention of living there "in affluence and honor." When he got to America, however, he did not know what to do with himself, and still less what to do with the inestimable pearls and diamonds of the Great Mogul. An ordinary pirate of romance would have escaped to the Spanish Main, but Avery did just what any realistic gentleman would do: after he had spent a short time in other cities — he concluded to go to Boston. The chronicler adds, "Arriving at Boston, he almost resolved to settle there." It was in the time of the Mathers. But in spite of its educational and religious advantages, Boston furnished no market for the gems of the Orient, so Captain Avery went to England. If he had in his youth read a few detective stories, he might have known how to get his jewels exchanged for the current coin of the realm; but his early education had been neglected, and he was of a singularly confiding and unsophisticated nature — when on land. After suffering from poverty he made the acquaintance of some wealthy merchants of Bristol, who took his gems on commission, on condition that they need not inquire how he came by them. That was the last Avery saw of the gems of the Great Mogul. A plain pirate was no match for financiers. Remittances were scanty, though promises were frequent. What came of it all? Nothing came of it; things simply dragged along. Avery was not hanged, neither did he get his money. At last, on a journey to Bristol to urge the merchants to a settlement, he fell sick and died. What became of the gems? Nobody knows. What became of those merchants of Bristol? Nobody cares. A novelist might, out of such material, make an ending quite clever and dreary.

To this realistic school of pirates belongs Thomas Veal, known in our history as the " Pirate of Lynn." To turn from the chapter on the Life, Atrocities, and Bloody Death of Black Beard to the chapter on the Lynn Pirate, is a relief to the overstrained sensibilities. Lynn is in the temperate zone, and we should naturally reason that its piracies would be more calm and equable than those of the tropics, and so they were. " On one pleasant evening, a little after sunset, a small vessel was seen to anchor near the mouth of the Saugus River. A boat was presently lowered from her side, into which four men descended and moved up the river." It is needless to say that these men were pirates. In the morning the vessel had disappeared, but a man found a paper whereon was a statement that if a quantity of shackles, handcuffs, and hatchets were placed in a certain nook, silver would be deposited near by to pay for them. The people of Lynn in those days were thrifty folk, and the hardware was duly placed in the spot designated, and the silver was found as promised. After some months four pirates came and settled in the woods. The historian declares it to be his opinion (and he speaks as an expert) that it would be impossible to select a place more convenient for a gang of pirates. He draws particular attention to the fact that the " ground was well selected for the cultivation of potatoes and common vegetables." This shows that the New England environment gave an industrial and agricultural cast to piracy which it has not had elsewhere.  In fact, after reading the whole chapter, I am struck by the pacific and highly moral character of these pirates.  The last of them — Thomas Veal — took up his abode in what is described as a " spacious cavern," about two miles from Lynn.  " There the fugitive fixed his residence, and practiced the trade of a shoemaker, occasionally coming down to the village to obtain articles of sustenance."  By uniting the occupations of market-gardening, shoe-making, and piracy, Thomas Veal managed to satisfy the demands of a frugal nature, and to live respected by his neighbors in Lynn.  It must have been a great alleviation in the lot of the small boys, when now and then they escaped from the eyes of the tithing-men, and in the cave listened to Mr. Veal singing his pirate's songs.  Of course a solo could give only a faint conception of what the full chorus would have been in the tropical forests, but still it must have curdled the blood to a very considerable extent.

There is, I must confess, a certain air of vagueness about this interesting narration.  No overt act of piracy is mentioned. Indeed, the evidence in regard to the piratical character of Mr. Veal, so far as it is given in this book, is largely circumstantial.

There is, first, the geographical argument. The Saugus River, being a winding stream, was admirably adapted for the resort of pirates who wished to prey upon the commerce of Boston and Salem. This establishes the opportunity and motive, and renders it antecedently probable that piracy was practiced. The river, it is said, was a good place in which to secrete boats. This we know from our reading was the invariable practice of pirates.

Another argument is drawn from the umbrageous character of the Lynn woods. We are told with nice particularity that in this tract of country " there were many thick pines, hemlocks, and cedars, and places where the rays of the sun at noon could not penetrate." Such a place would be just the spot in which astute pirates would be likely to bury their treasure, confident that it would never be discovered. The fact that nothing ever has been discovered here seems to confirm this supposition.

The third argument is that while a small cave still remains, the "spacious cavern" in which Thomas Veal, the piratical shoemaker, is said to have dwelt no longer exists. This clinches the evidence. For there was an earthquake in 1658. What more likely than that, in the earthquake, "the top of the rock was loosened and crushed down into the mouth of the cavern, inclosing the unfortunate inmate in its unyielding prison?" At any rate, there is no record of Mr. Veal or of his spacious cavern after that earthquake.

No one deserves to be called an antiquarian who cannot put two and two together, and reconstruct from these data a more or less elaborate history of the piracies of Mr. Thomas Veal. The only other explanation of the facts presented, that I can think of as having any degree of plausibility, is that possibly Mr. Veal may have been an Anabaptist, escaped from Boston, who imposed upon the people of Lynn by making them believe that he was only a pirate.

I must in candor admit that the Plutarch of piracy is sometimes more edifying than entertaining. He can never resist the temptation to draw a moral, and his dogmatic bias in favor of the doctrine of total depravity is only too evident. But his book has the great advantage that it is not devoid of incident. Take it all in all, there are worse books to read — after one is tired of reading books that are better.

I am inclined to think that our novelists must make home happy, or they may drive many of their readers to "The Pirate's Own Book." The policy of the absolute prohibition of romance, while excellent in theory, has practical difficulties in the way of enforcement. Perhaps, under certain restrictions, license might be issued to proper persons to furnish stimulants to the imagination. Of course the romancer should not be allowed to sell to minors, nor within a certain distance of a schoolhouse, nor to habitual readers. My position is the conservative one that commended itself to the judicious Rollo.

"'Well, Rollo,' said Dorothy, 'shall I tell you a true story, or one that is not true?'

"'I think, on the whole, Dorothy, I would rather have it true.'"

But there must have been times — though none are recorded — when Rollo tired even of the admirable clear thinking and precise information of

Jonas.   At such times he might have tolerated a story that was not so very true, if only it were interesting.   There are main thoroughfares paved with hard facts where the intellectual traffic must go on continually.   There are tracks on which, if a heedless child of romance should stray, he is in danger of being run down by the realists, those grim motor-men of the literary world.   But outside the congested districts there should be some roadways leading out into the open country where all things are still possible.   At the entrance to each of these roads there ought to be displayed the notice, " For pleasure only.   No heavy teaming allowed."   I should not permit any modern improvements in this district, but I should preserve all its natural features.   There should be not only a feudal castle with moat and drawbridge, but also a pirate's cave.

# The Honorable Points of Ignorance

⁓⦿⁓

I HAPPEN to live in a community where there is a deeply rooted prejudice in favor of intelligence, with many facilities for its advancement. I may, therefore, be looked upon as unmindful of my privileges when I confess that my chief pleasures have been found in the more secluded paths of ignorance.

I am no undiscriminating lover of Ignorance. I do not like the pitch-black kind which is the negation of all thought. What I prefer is a pleasant intellectual twilight, where one sees realities through an entrancing atmosphere of dubiety.

In visiting a fine old Elizabethan mansion in

the south of England our host took us to a room where he had discovered the evidences of a secret panel. "What is behind it?" we asked. "I do not know," he answered; "while I live it shall never be opened, for then I should have no secret chamber."

There was a philosopher after my own heart. He was wise enough to resist the temptation to sell his birthright of mystery for a mess of knowledge. The rural New Englander expresses his interest by saying, "I want to know!" But may one not have a real interest in persons and things which is free from inquisitiveness? For myself, I frequently prefer not to know. Were Bluebeard to do me the honor of intrusting me with his keys, I should spend a pleasant half-hour speculating on his family affairs. I might even put the key in the lock, but I do not think I should turn it. Why should I destroy twenty exciting possibilities for the sake of a single discovery?

I like to watch certain impressive figures as they cross the College Yard. They seem like the sages whom Dante saw: —

> "People were there with solemn eyes and slow,
> Of great authority in their countenance."

Do I therefore inquire their names, and intrusively seek to know what books they have written, before I admire their scholarship? No, to my old-fashioned way of thinking, scholarship is not a thing to be measured; it is a mysterious effluence. Were I to see —

> "Democritus who puts the world on chance,
> Diogenes, Anaxagoras, and Thales,
> Zeno, Empedocles, and Heraclitus,
>
> . . . . . . .
>
> Tully and Livy and moral Seneca,
> Euclid, geometrician, and Ptolemy,
> Galen, Hippocrates, and Avicenna,"

I should not care to ask, "Which is which?" still less should I venture to interview Galen on the subject of medicine, or put leading questions to Diogenes. The combined impression of ineffable wisdom would be more to me than any particular information I might get out of them.

But, as I said, I am not an enthusiast for Ignorance. Mine is not the zeal of a new convert, but the sober preference of one to the manner born. I do not look upon it as a panacea, nor, after the habit of reformers, would I insist that it should be taught in the public schools. There are important spheres wherein exact information is much to be preferred.

Because Ignorance has its own humble measure of bliss I would not jump at the conclusion that it is folly to be wise. That is an extravagant statement. If real wisdom were offered me I should accept it gratefully. Wisdom is an honorable estate, and, doubtless, it has pleasures of its own. I only have in mind the alternative that is usually presented to us, conscious ignorance or a kind of knowingness.

It is necessary, at this point, to make a distinction. A writer on the use of words has a chapter on Ignorantism, which is a term he uses to indicate Ignorance that mistakes itself, or seeks to make others mistake it, for Knowledge. For Ignorantism I make no plea. If Ignorance puts on a false uniform and is caught within the enemy's lines, it must suffer the penalties laid down in the laws of war.

Nor would I defend what Milton calls "the barbarous ignorance of the schools." This scholastic variety consists of the scientific definition and classification of "things that are n't so." It has no value except as a sort of gelatine culture for the propagation of verbal bacteria.

But the affectations of the pedants or the sciolists should not be allowed to cast discredit on the fair name of Ignorance. It is only natural Ignorance which I praise; not that which is acquired. It was a saying of Landor that if a man had a large mind he could afford to let the greater part of it lie fallow. Of course we small proprietors cannot do things on such a generous scale; but it seems to me that if one has only a little mind it is a mistake to keep it all under cultivation.

I hope that this praise of Ignorance may not give offense to any intelligent reader who may feel that he is placed by reason of his acquirements beyond the pale of our sympathies. He need fear no such exclusion. My Lady Ignorance is gracious and often bestows her choicest gifts on those who scorn her. The most erudite person is intelligent only in spots. Browning's Bishop Blougram questioned whether he should be called a skeptic or believer, seeing that he could only exchange

> "a life of doubt diversified by faith,
> For one of faith diversified by doubt:
> We called the chess-board white, — we call it black."

Whether a person thinks of his own intellectual state as one of knowledge diversified by ignorance or one of ignorance diversified by knowledge is a matter of temperament. We like him better when he frankly calls his intellectual chess-board black. That, at any rate, was the original color, the white is an afterthought.

Let me, then, without suspicion of treasonable intent, be allowed to point out what we may call in Shakespearean phrase "the honorable points of ignorance."

The social law against "talking shop" is an indication of the very widespread opinion that the exhibition of unmitigated knowledge is unseemly, outside of business hours. When we meet for pleasure we prefer that it should be on the humanizing ground of not knowing. Nothing is so fatal to conversation as an authoritative utterance. When a man who is capable of giving it enters,

> " All talk dies, as in a grove all song
> Beneath the shadow of a bird of prey."

Conversation about the weather would lose all its easy charm in the presence of the Chief of the Weather Bureau.

It is possible that the fear of exhibiting unusual information in a mixed company may be a survival of primitive conditions. Just as the domesticated dog will turn around on the rug before lying down, for hereditary reasons which I do not remember, so it is with civilized man. Once ignorance was universal and enforced by penalties. In the progress of the race the environment has been modified, but so strong is the influence of heredity that The Man Who Knows no sooner enters the drawing-room than he is seized by guilty fears. His ancestors for having exhibited a moiety of his intelligence were executed as wizards. But perhaps the ordinary working of natural selection may account for the facts. The law of the survival of the fittest admits of no exceptions, and the fittest to give us pleasure in conversation is the sympathetic person who appears to know very little more than we do.

In the commerce of ideas there must be reciprocity. We will not deal with one who insists that the balance of trade shall always be in his favor. Moreover there must be a spice of incertitude about the transaction. The real joy of

the intellectual traffic comes when we sail away
like the old merchant adventurers in search of
a market. There must be no prosaic bills of
exchange: it must be primitive barter. We
have a choice cargo of beads which we are
willing to exchange for frankincense and ivory.
If on some strange coast we should meet simple-
minded people who have only wampum, perhaps
even then we might make a trade.

Have you never when engaged in such commerce felt something of the spirit of the grave
Tyrian trader who had sailed away from the fre-
quented marts, and held on

" O'er the blue Midland waters with the gale,
    Betwixt the Syrtes and soft Sicily,
    To where the Atlantic raves
  Outside the western straits, and unbent sails
  There where down cloudy cliffs, through sheets of foam,
  Shy traffickers, the dark Iberians come ;
  And on the beach undid his corded bales."

It is not every day that one meets with such
shy traffickers, for the world is becoming very
sophisticated. One does not ask that those with
whom we converse should be ignorant of everything ; it is enough that they should not know
what is in our bales before we undo them.

One very serious drawback to our pleasure in conversation with a too well-informed person is the nervous strain that is involved. We are always wondering what will happen when he comes to the end of his resources. After listening to one who discourses with surprising accuracy upon any particular topic, we feel a delicacy in changing the subject. It seems a mean trick, like suddenly removing the chair on which a guest is about to sit down for the evening. With one who is interested in a great many things he knows little about there is no such difficulty. If he has passed the first flush of youth, it no longer embarrasses him to be caught now and then in a mistake; indeed your correction is welcomed as an agreeable interruption, and serves as a starting point for a new series of observations.

The pleasure of conversation is enhanced if one feels assured not only of wide margins of ignorance, but also of the absence of uncanny quickness of mind.

I should not like to be neighbor to a wit. It would be like being in proximity to a live wire. A certain insulating film of kindly stupidity is needed to give a margin of safety to human in-

tercourse. There are certain minds whose processes convey the impression of alternating currents of high voltage on a wire that is not quite
large enough for them. From such I would with-
draw myself.

One is freed from all such apprehensions in the
companionship of people who make no pretensions
to any kind of cleverness. "The laughter of
fools is like the crackling of thorns under a pot."
What cheerful sounds! The crackling of the dry
thorns! and the merry bubbling of the pot!

There is an important part played by what I
may call defensive Ignorance. It was said of
Robert Elsmere that he had a mind that was
defenseless against the truth. It is a fine thing
to be thus open to conviction, but the mental hospitality of one who is without prejudices is likely
to be abused. All sorts of notions importunately
demand attention, and he who thinks to examine
all their credentials will find no time left for his
own proper affairs.

For myself, I like to have a general reception-
room in my mind for all sorts of notions with
which I desire to keep up only a calling acquaint-

ance.   Here let them all be welcomed, good, bad,
and indifferent, in the spacious antechamber of
my Ignorance.   But I am not able to invite
them into my private apartments, for I am living
in a small way in cramped quarters, where there
is only room for my own convictions.   There are
many things that are interesting to hear about
which I do not care to investigate.   If one is
willing to give me the result of his speculations
on various esoteric doctrines I am ready to receive them in the spirit in which they are offered,
but I should not think of examining them closely;
it would be too much like looking a gift horse in
the mouth.

I should like to talk with a Mahatma about the
constitution of the astral body.   I do not know
enough about the subject to contradict his asser-
tions, and therefore he would have it all his own
way.   But were he to become insistent and ask
me to look into the matter for myself, I should
beg to be excused.   I would not take a single
step alone.   In such a case I agree with Sir
Thomas Browne that " it is better to sit down in
modest ignorance and rest contented with the
natural blessings of our own reasons."

There are zealous persons of a proselyting turn of mind who insist upon our accepting their ideas or giving reasons for our rejection of them. When we see the flames of controversy sweeping upon us, the only safety lies in setting a back fire which shall clear the ground of any fuel for argument. If we can only surround ourselves with a bare space of nescience we may rest in peace. I have seen a simple Chinese laundry-man, by adopting this plan, resist a storm of argument and invective without losing his temper or yielding his point. Serene, imperturbable, inscrutable, he stood undisturbed by the strife of tongues. He had one supreme advantage, — he did not know the language.

It was thus in the sixteenth century, when religious strife waxed mad around him, that Montaigne preserved a little spot of tolerant thought, "O what a soft, easy, and wholesome pillow is ignorance and incuriosity whereon to compose a well-contrived head!"

This sounds like mere Epicureanism, but Montaigne had much to say for himself: "Great abuse in the world is begot, or, to speak more boldly, all the abuses of the world are begot by our being taught to be afraid of professing our ignorance, and that we are bound to accept all things we are not able to refute. . . . They make me hate things that are likely when they impose upon me for infallible. I love those words which mollify and moderate the temerity of our propositions, ' Peradventure, in some sort, 't is said, I think,' and the like. . . . There is a sort of ignorance, strong and generous, that yields nothing in honor and courage to knowledge; an ignorance which to conceive requires no less knowledge than knowledge itself."

Not only is protection needed from the dogmatic assaults of our neighbors, but also from our own premature ideas. There are opinions which we are willing to receive on probation, but these probationers must be taught by judicious snubbing to know their place. The plausibilities and probabilities that are pleasantly received must not airily assume the place of certainties. Because you say to a stranger, " I 'm glad to see you," it is not certain that you are ready to sign his note at the bank.

When one happens to harbor any ideas of a radical character, he is fortunate if he is so constituted that it is not necessary for his self-respect that he should be cock-sure. The consciousness of the imperfection of his knowledge serves as a buffer when the train of progress starts with a jerk.

Sir Thomas More was, it is evident, favorably impressed with many of the sentiments of the gentleman from Utopia, but it was a great relief to him to be able to give them currency without committing himself to them. He makes no dogmatic assertion that the constitution of Utopia was better than that of the England of Henry VIII. In fact, he professes to know nothing about Utopia except from mere hearsay. He gracefully dismisses the subject, allowing the seeds of revolutionary ideas to float away on the thistle-down of polite Ignorance.

"When Raphael had made an end of speaking, though many things occurred to me both concerning the manners and laws of that country that seemed very absurd . . . yet since I perceived that Raphael was weary and I was not sure whether he could bear contradiction . . . I only commended their constitution and the account he had given of it in general; and so, taking him by

the hand, carried him to supper, and told him I
would find some other time for examining this
subject more particularly and discoursing more
copiously upon it."

One whose quiet tastes lead him away from the
main traveled roads into the byways of Ignorance
is likely to retain a feeling in regard to books
which belongs to an earlier stage of culture.
Time was when a book was a symbol of intellectual mysteries rather than a tool to be used.
When Omar Khayyám sang of the delights of a
jug of wine and a book, I do not think he was
intemperate in the use of either. The same book
and the same jug of wine would last him a long
time. The chief thing was that it gave him a
comfortable feeling to have them within reach.

The primitive feeling in regard to a book as a
kind of talisman survives chiefly among biblio-
philes, but with them it is overlaid by matters of
taste which are quite beyond the comprehension
of ordinary people. As for myself, I know nothing of such niceties.

I know nothing of rare bindings or fine edi-
tions. My heart is never disturbed by coveting

the contents of my neighbor's bookshelves. Indeed, I have always listened to the tenth commandment with a tranquil heart since I learned,
in the Shorter Catechism, that " the tenth commandment forbiddeth all discontentment with
our own estate, envying or grieving at the good
of our neighbor and all inordinate motions and
affections to anything that is his." If that be all,
it is not aimed at me, particularly in this matter
of books.

I feel no discontentment at the disorderly array
of bound volumes that I possess. I know that
they are no credit either to my taste or to my
scholarship, but if that offends my neighbor, the
misery is his, not mine. If he should bring a
railing accusation against me, let him remember
that there is a ninth commandment which " forbiddeth anything that is injurious to our own or
our neighbor's good name." As for any inordinate motions or affections toward his literary
treasures, I have no more than toward his choice
collection of stamps.

Yet I have one weakness in common with the
bibliophile; I have a liking for certain books
which I have neither time nor inclination to read.

Just as according to the mediæval theory there was a sanctity about a duly ordained clergyman altogether apart from his personal character, so there is to my mind an impressiveness about some volumes which has little to do with their contents, or at least with my knowledge of them. Why should we be too curious in regard to such matters? There are books which I love to see on the shelf. I feel that virtue goes out of them, but I should think it undue familiarity to read them.

The persons who have written on "Books that have helped me" have usually confined their list to books which they have actually read. One book has clarified their thoughts, another has stimulated their wills, another has given them useful knowledge. But are there no Christian virtues to be cultivated? What about humility, that pearl of great price?

To be constantly reminded that you have not read Kant's "Critique of the Pure Reason," and that therefore you have no right to express a final opinion on philosophy, does not that save you from no end of unnecessary dogmatism? The silent monitor with its accusing, uncut pages is a blessed help to the meekness of wisdom. A

book that has helped me is "The History of
the Rebellion and Civil Wars of England," by
Edward, Earl of Clarendon. I am by nature and
education a Cromwellian, of a rather narrow type.
I am more likely than not to think of Charles I.
as a man of sin. When, therefore, I brought
home Clarendon's History I felt a glow of conscious virtue; the volume was an outward and
visible sign of inward and spiritual grace, — the
grace of tolerance; and so it has ever been to me.

Years have passed, and the days of leisure have
not yet come when I could devote myself to the
reading of it. Perhaps the fact that I discovered
that the noble earl's second sentence contains
almost three hundred words may have had a dis-
couraging influence, — but we will let that pass.
Because I have not crossed the Rubicon of the
second chapter, will you say that the book has
not influenced me? "When to the sessions of
sweet, silent thought," with the Earl of Clarendon,
"I summon up remembrance of things past," is it
necessary that I should laboriously turn the pages?
It is enough that I feel my prejudices oozing
away, and that I am convinced, when I look at
the much prized volume, that there are two sides

to this matter of the English Commonwealth. Could the most laborious reading do more for me?

Indeed, it is dangerous, sometimes, not to let well-enough alone. Wordsworth's fickle Muse gave him several pretty fancies about the unseen banks of Yarrow. "Yarrow Unvisited" was so delightful that he was almost tempted to be content with absent treatment.

> "We will not see them, will not go
> To-day nor yet to-morrow,
> Enough if in our hearts we know
> There 's such a place as Yarrow.
> Be Yarrow's stream unseen, unknown,
> It must, or we shall rue it,
> We have a vision of our own,
> Ah, why should we undo it ? "

Ah, why, indeed? the reader asks, after reading Yarrow Visited and Yarrow Re-visited. The visits were a mistake.

Perhaps Clarendon Unread is as good for my soul as Clarendon Read or Clarendon Re-read. Who can tell?

There is another sphere in which the honorable points of ignorance are not always sufficiently appreciated, that of Travel. The pleasure of staying at home consists in being surrounded by things which are familiar and which we know all about. The primary pleasure of going abroad consists in the encounter with the unfamiliar and the unknown.

That was the impulse which stirred old Ulysses to set forth once more upon his travels.

> " For my purpose holds
> To sail beyond the sunset, and the baths
> Of all the western stars, until I die.
> It may be that the gulfs will wash us down,
> It may be we shall touch the Happy Isles,
> And see the great Achilles, whom we knew."

" It may be " — there lay the charm. There was no knowing what might happen on the dark, broad seas. Perhaps they might get lost, and then again they might come upon the Happy Isles. And if as they sailed under their looming shores they should see the great Achilles — why all the better!

What joys the explorers of the New World experienced! The heart leaps up at the very title of Sebastian Cabot's joint stock company. "Merchants Adventurers of England for the discovery

of lands, territories, isles and signories, unknown."
There was no knowing beforehand which was an
island and which the mainland.   All they had to
do was to keep on, sure only of finding something
which they had not expected.   When they got to
the mainland they were as likely as not to stumble
on the great Khan himself.   Of course they might
not make a discovery of the first magnitude like
that of the Spaniards on the Peak in Darien, —
but if it was not one thing it was another !

Two or three miles back of Plymouth, Mass.,
is a modest little pond called Billington's Sea.
Billington, an adventurous Pilgrim, had climbed
a tree, and looking westwards had caught sight
of the shimmering water.   He looked at it with
a wild surmise, and then the conviction flashed
upon him that he had discovered the goal of
hardy mariners, — the great South Sea.   That
was a great moment for Billington !

Of course the Spaniards were more fortunate
in their geographical position.   It turned out
that it was the Pacific that they saw from their
Peak in Darien ; while Billington's Sea does not
grow on acquaintance.

But my heart goes out to Billington.   He also

was a discoverer, according to his lights. He belonged to a hardy breed, and could stare on new scenes with the best of them. It was not his fault that the Pacific was not there. If it had been, Billington would have discovered it. We know perfectly well that the Pacific Ocean does not lave the shores of Plymouth County, and so we should not go out into the woods on a fine morning to look for it. There is where Billington had the advantage of us.

Is it not curious that while we profess to envy the old adventurers the joys of discovery, yet before we set out on our travels we make it a point of convenience to rob ourselves of these possibilities? Before we set out for Ultima Thule we must know precisely where it is, and how we are going to get there, and what we are to see and what others have said about it. After a laborious course of reading the way is as familiar to our minds as the road to the post office. After that there is nothing more for us to do but to sally forth to verify the guide-books. We have done all that we could to brush the bloom off our native Ignorance.

Of course even then all the possibilities of

discovery are not shut out. The best-informed person cannot be completely guarded against surprise. Accidents will happen, and there is always the chance that one may have been misinformed.

I remember a depressed looking lady whom I encountered as she trudged through the galleries of the Vatican with grim conscientiousness. She had evidently a stern duty to perform for the cause of Art. But in the Sistine Chapel the stillness was broken by her voice, which had a note of triumph as she spoke to her daughter. She had discovered an error in Baedeker. It infused new life into her tired soul.

"Some flowerets of Eden we still inherit
Though the trail of the serpent is over them all."

Speaking of the Vatican, that suggests the weak point in my argument. It suggests that there are occasions when knowledge is very convenient. On the Peak in Darien the first comer, with the wild surmise of ignorance, has the advantage in the quality of his sensation; but it is different in Jerusalem or Rome. There the pleasure consists in the fact that a great many interesting people have been there before and done many interesting things, which it might be well to know about.

At this point I am quite willing to grant an inch; with the understanding that it shall not be lengthened into an ell. The Camel of Knowledge may push his head into the tent, and we shall have to resist his further encroachments as we may.

What we call the historic sense is not consistent with a state of nescience. The picture which the eye takes in is incomplete without the thousand associations which come from previous thought. Still, it remains true that the finest pleasure does not come when the mental images are the most precise. Before entering Paradise the mediæval pilgrims tasted of the streams of Eunoë and Lethe, — the happy memory and the happy forgetfulness. The most potent charm comes from the judicious mingling of these waters.

There is a feeling of antiquity that only comes now and then, but which it is worth traveling far to experience. It is the thrill that comes when we consciously stand in the presence of the remote past. Some scene brings with it an impression of immemorial time. In almost every case we find that it comes from being reminded of something which we have once known and more than half forgotten. What are the "mists of time" but imperfect memories?

Modern psychologists have given tardy recognition to the "Subliminal Self," — the self that lodges under the threshold of consciousness. He is a shy gnome, and loves the darkness rather than the light; not, as I believe, because his deeds are evil, but for reasons best known to himself. To all appearances he is the most ignorant fellow in the world, and yet he is no fool. As for the odds and ends that he stores up under the threshold, they are of more value than the treasures that the priggish Understanding displays in his show windows upstairs.

In traveling through historic lands the Subliminal Self overcomes his shyness. There are scenes and even words that reach back into hoar antiquity, and bring us into the days of eld.

Each person has his own chronology. If I were to seek to bring to mind the very ancientest time, I should not think of the cave-dwellers: I should repeat, "The Kenites, the Kenizzites,

the Kadmonites, the Hittites, the Perizzites, the
Amorites, the Canaanites, the Girgashites."

There is antiquity! It is not only a long time
since these tribes dwelt in the land; it has been
a long time since I first heard of them.

My memory goes back to the time when a dis-
consolate little boy sat on a bench in a Sunday-
school and asked himself, "What is a Girgashite?"

The habit of the Sunday-school of mingling
the historical and ethical elements in one inextri-
cable moral had made it uncertain whether the
Girgashite was a person or a sin. In either case
it happened a long time ago. There upon the
very verge of Time stood the Girgashite, like the
ghost in Ossian, "His spear was a column of
mist, and the stars looked dim through his form."

Happily my studies have not led in that direction, and there is nothing to disturb the first
impression. If some day wandering over Oriental hills I should come upon some broken
monuments of the Girgashites, I am sure that
I should feel more of a thrill than could possibly
come to my more instructed companion. To him
it would be only the discovery of another fact, to

fit into his scheme of knowledge : to me it would
be like stumbling unawares into the primeval
world.

What is more delightful than in a railway
train in Italy to hear voices in the night calling
out names that recall the lost arts of our child-
hood ! There is a sense

> " Of something here like something there,
> Of something done, I know not where,
> Such as no language can declare."

There is a bittersweet to it, for there is a momentary fear that you may be called upon to con-
strue ; but when that is past it is pure joy.

"Monte Soracte," said the Italian gentleman
on the train between Foligno and Rome, as he
pointed out a picturesque eminence. My an-
swering smile was intended to convey the impression that one touch of the classics makes the
whole world kin. Had I indeed kept up my
Horace, a host of clean-cut ideas would have instantly rushed into my mind. " Is that Soracte !
It is not what I had reason to expect. As a
mountain I prefer Monadnock."

Fortunately I had no such prepossessions. I
had expected nothing. There only came impres-

sions of lessons years ago in a dingy school-room presided over by a loved instructor whom we knew as " Prof. Ike." Looking back through the mists of time, I felt that I had been the better for having learned the lessons, and none the worse for having long since forgotten them. In those days Soracte had been a noun standing in mysterious relations to a verb unknown ; but now it was evident that it was a mountain. There it stood under the clear Italian sky just as it had been in the days of Virgil and Horace. Thoughts of Horace and of the old professor mingled pleasantly so long as the mountain was in sight.

It may seem to some timid souls that this praise of Ignorance may have a sinister motive, and may be intended to deter from the pursuit of knowledge. On the contrary, it is intended to encourage those who are " faint yet pursuing."

It must have occurred to every serious person that the pursuit of knowledge is not what it once was. Time was when to know seemed the easiest thing in the world. All that a man had to do was to assert dogmatically that a thing was so, and then argue it out with some one who had even less acquaintance with the subject than he had. He was not hampered by a rigid, scientific method, nor did he need to make experiments, which after all might not strengthen his position. The chief thing was a certain tenacity of opinion which would enable him, in Pope's phrase, to " hold the eel of science by the tail." There were no troublesome experts to cast discredit on this slippery sport. If a man had a knack at metaphysics and a fine flow of technical language he could satisfy all reasonable curiosity about the Universe. Or with the minimum of effort he might attain a jovial scholarship adequate for all convivial purposes, like Chaucer's pilgrim

> " Whan that he wel dronken had the win,
> Than wold he speken no word but Latin."

It was the golden age of the amateur, when certainty could be had for the asking, and one could stake out any part of the wide domain of human interest and hold it by the right of squatter sovereignty. But in these days the man who aspires to know must do something more than assert his conviction. He must submit to all sorts of mortifying tests, and at best he can obtain a title to only the tiniest bit of the field he covets.

With the severer definitions of knowledge and the delimitation of the territory which any one may call his own there has come a curious result. While the aggregate of intellectual wealth has increased, the individual workers are being reduced to penury. It is a pathetic illustration of Progress and Poverty. The old and highly respected class of gentlemen and scholars is being depleted. Scholarship has become so difficult that those who aspire after it have little time for the amenities. It is not as it was in the "spacious times of great Elizabeth." Enter any company of modern scholars and ask what they know about any large subject, and you will find that each one hastens to take the poor debtor's oath. How can they be expected to know so much?

On this minute division of intellectual labor the exact sciences thrive, but conversation, poetry, art, and all that belongs to the humanities languish.

Your man of highly specialized intelligence has often a morbid fear of half-knowledge, and he does not dare to express an opinion that has not been the result of original research. He shuns the innocent questioners who would draw him out, as if they were so many dunning credit-ors. He becomes a veritable Dick Swiveller as one conversational thoroughfare after another is closed against him, until he no longer ventures abroad. The worst of it is that he has a haunt-ing apprehension that even the bit of knowledge which he calls his own may be taken away from him by some new discovery, and he may be cast adrift upon the Unknowable.

It is then that he should remember the wisdom of the unjust steward, so that when he is cast out of the House of Knowledge he may find con-genial friends in the habitations of Ignorance.

There are a great many mental activities that stop short of strict knowledge. Where we do not know, we may imagine, and hope, and dare ; we may laugh at our neighbor's mistakes, and occasionally at our own. We may enjoy the delicious moments of suspense when we are on the verge of finding out; and if it should happen that the discovery is postponed, then we have a chance to go over the delightful process again.

To say " I do not know " is not nearly as

painful as it seems to those who have not tried it.  The active mind, when the conceit of absolute knowledge has been destroyed, quickly recovers itself and cries out, after the manner of Brer Rabbit when Brer Fox threw him into the brier patch, " Bred en bawn in a brier patch, Brer Fox — bred en bawn in a brier patch!"

# That History should be Readable

**T**HAT was a clever device which a writer of "mere literature" hit upon when he boldly dedicated his book to a man of prodigious learning. "Who so guarded," he says, "can suspect his safety even when he travels through the Enemy's Country, for such is the vast field of Learning, where the Learned (though not numerous enough to be an Army) lie in small Parties, maliciously in Ambush, to destroy all New Men who look into their Quarters."

It is doubtful, however, whether in these days a lover of Ignorance — or, if you prefer, an ignorant lover of good things — could be safe in the enemy's country, even under the protection of

such a Mr. Great Heart.    It is no longer true
that the Learned are not numerous enough to be
an army and are content with guerrilla warfare ;
on the contrary, they have increased to multitudes, and their well-disciplined forces hold all
the strategic points.    As for those who love to
read and consider, rather than to enter into
minute researches, it is as in the days of Sham-
gar, the son of Anoth, when " the highways were
unoccupied and the people walked through byways."

There is one field, however, that the Gentle
Reader will not give up without a struggle — it
is that of history.    He claims that it belongs to
Literature as much as to Science.    History and
Story are variations of the same word, and the
historian who is master of his art must be a story-
teller.    Clio was not a school-mistress, but a
Muse, and the papyrus roll in her hand does not
contain mere dates and statistics, it is filled with
the record of heroic adventures.    The primitive
form of history was verbal tradition, as one
generation told the story of the past to the
generation that followed.

" There was a great advantage in that method,"

says the Gentle Reader, "the irrelevant details
dropped out.   It is only the memorable things
that can be remembered.   What a pleasant invitation that was in the eighty-first psalm to the
study of Hebrew History, in order to learn what
had happened when Israel went out through the
land of Egypt: —

> 'Take up the psalm and bring hither the timbrel,
> The pleasant harp with the psaltery,
> Blow up the trumpet in the new moon,
> And the full moon on our solemn feast days.'

"The Jews had a way of setting their history to
music, and bringing in the great events as a glorious refrain, which they never feared repeating
too often; perhaps that is one reason why their
history has lasted so long."

The Gentle Reader's liking for histories that
might be read to the accompaniment of the
"pleasant harp and psaltery," and which now
and then stir him as with the sound of a trumpet,
brings upon him many a severe rebuke.   He is
told that his favorite writers are frequently inac-
curate and one-sided.   The true historian, he is
informed, is a prodigy of impartiality, who has
divested himself of all human passions, in order

that he may set down in exact sequence the course of events. The Gentle Reader turns to these highly praised volumes and finds himself adrift, without human companionship, on a bottomless sea of erudition, — writings, writings everywhere and not a page to read! Returning from this perilous excursion, he ever after adheres to his original predilection for histories that are readable.

He is of the opinion that a history must be essentially a work of the imagination. This does not mean that it must not be true, but it means that the important truth about any former generation can only be reproduced through the imagination. The important thing is that these people were once alive. No critical study of their meagre memorials can make us enter into their joys, their griefs, and their fears. The memorials only suggest to the historic imagination what the reality must have been.

Peter Bell could recognize a fact when he saw it : —

> " A primrose on the river's brim
> A yellow primrose was to him,
> And it was nothing more."

As long as the primrose was there, he could be trusted to describe it accurately enough.   But set Peter Bell the task of describing last year's primrose.   "There are n't any last year's primroses on the river's brim," says Peter, "so you must be content with a description of the one in my herbarium.   Last year's primroses, you will observe, are very much flattened out."   To Mr. Peter Bell, after he has spent many years in the universities, a document is a document, and it is nothing more.   When he has compared a great many documents, and put them together in a mechanical way, he calls his work a history. That 's where he differs from the Gentle Reader who calls it only the crude material out of which a man of genius may possibly make a history.

To the Gentle Reader it is a profoundly interesting reflection that since this planet has been inhabited people have been fighting, and working, and loving, and hating, with an intensity born of the conviction that, if they went at it hard enough, they could finish the whole business in one generation.   He likes to get back into any one of these generations just "to get the feel of it."   He does not care so much for the final summing up of the process, as to see it in the making. Any one who can give him that experience is his friend.

He is interested in the stirring times of the English Revolution, and goes to the historical expert to find what it was all about. The historical expert starts with the Magna Charta and makes a preliminary survey. Then he begins his march down the centuries, intrenching every position lest he be caught unawares by the critics. His intellectual forces lack mobility, as they must wait for their baggage trains. At last he comes to the time of the Stuarts, and there is much talk of the royal prerogative, and ship money, and attainders, and acts of Parliament. There are exhaustive arguments, now on the one side and now on the other, which exactly balance one another. There are references to bulky volumes, where at the foot of every page the notes run along, like little angry dogs barking at the text.

The Gentle Reader calls out: "I have had enough of this. What I want to know is what it's all about, and which side, on the whole, has the right of it. Which side are you on? Are you a Roundhead or a Cavalier? Are your sympathies with the Whigs or the Tories?"

"Sympathies!" says the expert. "Who ever heard of a historian allowing himself to sympathize? I have no opinions of my own to present. My great aim is not to prejudice the mind of the student."

"Nonsense," says the Gentle Reader; "I am not a student, nor is this a school-room. It's all in confidence; speak out as one gentleman to another under a friendly roof! What do you think about it? No matter if you make a mistake or two, I'll forget most that you say, anyway. All that I care for is to get the gist of the matter. As for your fear of warping my mind, there's not the least danger in the world. My mind is like a tough bit of hickory; it will fly back into its original shape the moment you let go. I have a hundred prejudices of my own, — one more won't hurt me. I want to know what it was that set the people by the ears. Why did they cut off the head of Charles I., and why did they drive out James II.? I can't help thinking that there must have been something more exciting than those discussions of yours about constitutional theories. Do you know, I sometimes doubt whether most of the people who went to the wars knew that there was such a thing as the English Constitution ; the subject had n't been written up then. I suspect that something happened that was not set down in your book; something that made those people fighting mad."

Then the Gentle Reader turns to his old and much criticised friend Macaulay, and asks, —

" What do you think about it ? "

" Think about it ! " says Macaulay. " I 'll tell you what I think about it. To begin with, that Charles I., though good enough as a family man, was a consummate liar."

" That 's the first light I 've had on the subject," says the Gentle Reader. " Charles lied, and that made the people mad ? "

" Precisely ! I perceive that you have the historic sense. We English can't abide a liar ; so at last when we could not trust the king's word we chopped off his head. Mind you, I 'm not defending the regicides, but between ourselves I don't mind saying that I think it served him right. At any rate our blood was up, and there was no stopping us. I wish I had time to tell

you all about Hampden, and Pym, and Crom-
well, but I must go on to the glorious year 1688,
and tell you how it all came about, and how we
sent that despicable dotard, James, flying across
the Channel, and how we brought in the good
and wise King William, and how the great line
of Whig statesmen began. I take for granted —
as you appear to be a sensible man — that you
are a Whig ? "

" I 'm open to conviction," says the Gentle
Reader.

In a little while he is in the very thick of it.
He is an Englishman of the seventeenth century.
He has taken sides and means to fight it out. He
knows how to vote on every important question
that comes before Parliament. No Jacobite soph-
istry can beguile him. When William lands
he throws up his hat, and after that he stands by
him, thick or thin. When you tell him that he
ought to be more dispassionate in his historical
judgments, he answers : " That would be all very
well if we were not dealing with living issues, —
but with Ireland in an uproar and the Papists
ready to swarm over from France, there is a call
for decision. A man must know his own mind.

You may stand off and criticise William's policy; but the question is, What policy do you propose? You say that I have not exhausted the subject, and that there are other points of view. Very likely. Show me another point of view, only make it as clear to me as Macaulay makes his. Let it be a real view, and not a smudge. Some other day I may look at it, but I must take one thing at a time. What I object to is the historian who takes both sides in the same paragraph. That is what I call offensive bi-partisanship."

The Gentle Reader is interested not only in what great men actually were, but in the way they appeared to those who loved or hated them. He is of the opinion that the legend is often more significant than the colorless annals. When a legend has become universally accepted and has lived a thousand years, he feels that it should be protected in its rights of possession by some statute of limitation. It has come to have an independent life of its own. He has, therefore, no sympathy with Gibbon in his identification of St. George of England with George of Cappadocia, a dishonest army contractor who supplied the troops of the Emperor Julian with bacon.

Says Gibbon: "His employment was mean; he rendered it infamous. He accumulated wealth by the basest arts of fraud and corruption; but his malversations were so notorious that George was compelled to escape from the pursuit of his enemies. . . . This odious stranger, disguising every circumstance of time and place, assumed the mask of a martyr, a saint, and a Christian hero; and the infamous George of Cappadocia has been transformed into the renowned St. George of England, the patron of arms, of chivalry, and of the garter."

"That is a serious indictment," says the Gentle Reader. "I have no plea to make for the Cappadocian; I can readily believe that his bacon was bad. But why not let bygones be bygones? If he managed to transform himself into a saint, and for many centuries avoid all suspicion, I believe that it was a thorough reformation. St. George of England has long been esteemed as a valiant gentleman, — and, at any rate, that affair with the dragon was greatly to his credit."

Sometimes the Gentle Reader is disturbed by finding that different lines of tradition have been mixed, and his mind becomes the battleground

whereon old blood feuds are fought out.  Thus
it happens that as a child he was brought up on
the tales of the Covenanters and imbibed their
stern resentment against their persecutors.  He
learned to hate the very name of Graham of
Claverhouse who brought desolation upon so many
innocent homes.  On the other hand, his heart
beats high when he hears the martial strains of
Bonnie Dundee.  "There was a man for you!"

> "Dundee he is mounted, he rides up the street,
>   The bells are rung backward, the drums they are beat.
>
> .   .   .   .   .   .   .   .   .
>
> 'Away to the hills, to the caves, to the rocks —
>   Ere I own a usurper, I 'll couch with the fox!
>   And tremble, false Whigs, in the midst of your glee,
>   You have not seen the last of my bonnet and me! '
>
> .   .   .   .   .   .   .   .   .
>
> He waved his proud hand, and the trumpets were blown,
>   The kettle-drums clashed, and the horsemen rode on,
>   Till on Ravelston's cliffs and on Clermeston's lee
>   Died away the wild war notes of Bonnie Dundee."

"When I see him wave his proud hand," says
the Gentle Reader, "I am his clansman, and I 'm
ready to be off with him."

"I thought you were a Whig," says the student of history.

"I thought so too, — but what 's politics where

the affections are enlisted? Don't you hear those wild war notes?"

"But are you aware that the Bonnie Dundee is the same man whom you have just been denouncing under the name of Graham of Claverhouse?"

"Are you sure they are the same?" sighs the Gentle Reader. "I cannot make them seem the same. To me there are two of them: Graham of Claverhouse, whom I hate, and the Bonnie Dundee, whom I love. If it's all the same to you, I think I shall keep them separate and go on loving and hating as aforetime."

But though the Gentle Reader has the defects of his qualities and is sometimes led astray by his sympathies, do not think that he is altogether lacking in solidity of judgment. He has a genuine love of truth and finds it more interesting than fiction — when it is well written. If he objects to the elimination of myth and fable it is because he is profoundly interested in the history of human feeling. The story that is the embodiment of an emotion is itself of the greatest significance. In Shelley's Prometheus Unbound,

before Jupiter himself is revealed, the Phantasm
of Jupiter appears and speaks.   Prometheus
addresses him : —

> " Tremendous Image, as thou art must be
> He whom thou shadowest forth."

On the stage of history each great personage has
a phantasmal counterpart; sometimes there are
many of them.   Each phantasm becomes a centre
of love and hate.

The cold-blooded historian gives us what he
calls the real Napoleon.   He is, he asserts, neither the Corsican Ogre of the British imagination nor the Heroic Emperor for whom myriads
of Frenchmen gladly died.   Perhaps not; but
when the Napoleonic legend has been banished,
what about the Napoleonic wars?   The Phantasms of Napoleon appear on every battlefield.
The men of that day saw them, and were nerved
to the conflict.   The reader must, now and then,
see them, or he can have no conception of what
was going on.   He misses " the moving why they
did it."   And as for the real Napoleon, what was
the magic by which he was able to call such
phantasms from the vasty deep ?

The careful historian who would trace the history of Europe in the centuries that followed the barbarian invasion is sorely troubled by the intrusion of legendary elements. After purging his work of all that savors of romance, he has a very neat and connected narrative.

"But is it true?" asks the Gentle Reader. "I for one do not believe it. The course of true history never did run so smooth. Here is a worthy person who undertakes to furnish me with an idea of the Dark Ages, and he forgets the principal fact, which is that it was dark. His picture has all the sharp outlines of a noonday street scene. I don't believe he ever spent a night alone in a haunted house. If he had he would have known that if you don't see ghosts, you see shapes that look like them. At midnight mysterious forms loom large. The historian must have a genius for depicting Chaos. He must make me dimly perceive ' the fragments of forgotten peoples,' with their superstitions, their formless fears, their vague desires. They were all fighting them in the dark.

> " ' For friend and foe were shadows in the mist,
>    And friend slew friend not knowing whom he slew;
>    And some had visions out of golden youth,

> And some beheld the faces of old ghosts
> Look in upon the battle; and in the mist
> Was many a noble deed, many a base
> And chance and craft and strength in single fights,
> And ever and anon with host to host
> Shocks, and the splintering spear, the hard mail hewn,
> Shield-breakings, and the clash of brands, the crash
> Of battle axes on shattered helms, and shrieks
> After the Christ, of those who falling down
> Looked up for heaven and only saw the mist.'"

"But, Gentle Reader," says the Historian, "that is poetry, not history."

"Perhaps it is, but it's what really happened."

He is of the opinion that many histories owe their quality of unreadableness to the virtues of their authors. The kind-hearted historians overload their works through their desire to rescue as many events and persons as possible from oblivion. When their better judgment tells them that they should be off, they remain to drag in one more. Alas, their good intention defeats itself; their frail craft cannot bear the added burden, and all hands go to the bottom. There is no surer oblivion than that which awaits one whose name is recorded in a book that undertakes to tell all.

The trouble with facts is that there are so many
of them.   Here are millions of happenings every
day.  Each one has its infinite series of antecedents
and consequents; and each takes longer in the
telling than in the doing.  Evidently there must
be some principle of selection.   Naturalists with
a taste for mathematics tell us of the appalling
catastrophe which would impend if every codfish
were to reach maturity.   It would be equaled by
the state of things which would exist were every
incident duly chronicled.   A foretaste of this
calamity has been given in our recent war, — and
yet there were some of our military men who did
not write reminiscences.

What the principle of selection shall be depends
upon the predominant interest of the writer.
But there must be a clear sequence ; one can relate only what is related to the chosen theme.
The historian must reverse the order of natural
evolution and proceed from the heterogeneous to
the homogeneous.   Alas for the ill-fated pundit
who, forgetting his aim, flounders in the bottomless morass of heterogeneity.   The moment he
begins to tell how things are he remembers some
incongruous incident which proves that they were

quite otherwise. The genius for narrative consists in the ability to pick out the facts which
belong together and which help each other along.
The company must keep step, and the stragglers
must be mercilessly cut off. One cannot say of
any fact that it is important in itself. The important thing is that which has a direct bearing
on the subject. The definition of dirt as matter
in the wrong place is suggestive. All the details
that throw light on the main action are of value.
Those that obscure it are but petty dust. It is
no sufficient plea that the dust is very real and
that it took a great deal of trouble to collect
it.

As vivid a bit of history as one may read is the
Journal of Sally Wister, a Quaker girl who lived
near Philadelphia during the period of the American Revolution. She gives a narrative of the
things which happened to her during those fate-
ful years. In October, 1777, she says, " Here, my
dear, passes an interval of several weeks in which
nothing happened worth the time and paper it
would take to write it."

The editor is troubled at this remark, because
during that very week the Battle of Germantown

had been fought not far away.  But Sally Wister
had the true historical genius.  The Battle of
Germantown was an event, and so was the coming
of a number of gay young officers to the hospitable
country house; and this latter event was much
more important to Sally Wister.  So omitting all
irrelevant incidents, she gives a circumstantial
account of what was happening on the centre of
the stage.

"Cousin Prissa and myself were sitting at the
door; I in my green skirt, dark gown, etc.  Two
genteel men of the military order rode up to the
door.  'Your servant, ladies,' etc.  Asked if they
could have quarters for General Smallwood."

"I can see just how they did it," says the
Gentle Reader, "and what a commotion the
visit made.  Now when a person who is just as
much absorbed in the progress of the Revolutionary War as Sally Wister was in those young
officers writes about it I will read his history
gladly."

Some otherwise excellent histories fall into the
abyss of unreadableness because of the author's
unnecessary pains to justify his heroes to the

critical intelligence of the reader.  He is continually making apologies when he should be telling a story.  He is comparing the deeds of one
age with the ethical standards of another; and
the result is a series of moral anachronisms.
There is a running fire of more or less irrelevant
comment.

What a delightful plan that was, which the
author of the Book of Judges hit upon to
avoid this difficulty!  He had a hard task.  His
worthies were not persons of settled habits, and
they did many things that might appear shocking
to later generations.  They were called upon to
do rough work and they did it in their own way.
If the author had undertaken to justify their conduct by any conventional standard he would have
made sorry work of it.  What he did was much
better than that.  Whenever he came to a point
where there was danger of the mind of the reader
becoming turbid with moral reflections that belonged to a later age, he threw in the clarifying
suggestion, " And there was no King in Israel,
and every man did what was right in his own
eyes."  This precipitated all the disturbing elements, and the story ran on swift and clear.  It

was as if when the reader was about to protest the author anticipated him with, " What would you do, reader, if the Philistines were upon you and there were no King in Israel ? " Undoubtedly under such circumstances it would be a great relief to catch sight of Gideon or Samson. It would not be a time for fastidiousness about their shortcomings; they would be hailed as strong deliverers.

" That is just the point of it," cries the Gentle Reader. " They were on our side. The important thing is to recognize our friends. To teach us who our friends are is the purpose of history. Here is a conflict that has been going on for ages. The men who have done valiant service are not all smooth-spoken gentlemen in black coats — but what of it ? They have done what they could. We can't say that each act was absolutely right, but they were moving in the right direction. When a choice was offered they took the better part. The historian should not only know what they did, but what was the alternative offered them. There was the Prophet Samuel. Some persons will have no further respect for him after they learn that he hewed

Agag in pieces before the Lord. They think he
ought to have stood up for Free Religion. They
take for granted that the alternative offered him
was religious toleration as we understand it. It
was nothing of the sort. The question for a man
of that age was, Shall Samuel hew Agag in pieces,
or shall Agag hew Samuel in pieces, and my
sympathies are with Samuel."

Having once made allowance for the differences of time and place, he follows with eager
interest the fortunes of the men who have made
the world what it is. What if they do have their
faults? He does not care for what he calls New
England Primer style of History : —

> "Young Obadias, David, Josias
> All were pious."

Such monotony of excellence wearies him, and
the garment of praise is accompanied by a spirit
of heaviness.

"I like saints best in the state of nature," he
says; "the process of canonization does not seem
good for them. When too many of them are
placed together in a book their virtues kill one
another, and at a little distance all halos look
very much alike."

There are certain histories which he finds read-able, not because he cares very much for their ostensible subject, but because of the light they throw on the author's personality. He, good man, thinks he is telling the story of the Carlo-vingian Dynasty, or the rise of the Phœnician sea power, while in reality he is giving an intimate account of his own state of mind. The author is like a bee which wanders far afield and visits many flowers, but always brings back the spoil to one hollow tree. The Gentle Reader, like a practiced bee hunter, is careless of the outward journeys, but watches closely the direction of the return flight.

"If you would know a person's limitations," he says, "induce him to write on some large subject like the History of Civilization, or the History of the Origin and Growth of the Moral Sentiment. You will find his particular hobby writ large."

He takes up a History of the Semites. "What a pertinacious fellow he is," alluding not to any ancient Semite but to the Author, "how closely he sticks to his point! He has discovered a new fact about the Amalekites, — I wonder what he will do with it. Just as I expected! there he is back with it to that controversy he is having with his Presbytery. I notice that he calls the children of Israel the Beni-Israel. He knows that that sort of thing irritates the conservative party. It suggests that he is following Renan, and yet it may only prove that he thinks in Hebrew."

The Gentle Reader regards ambitious works on the Philosophy of History with mingled suspicion and curiosity. So much depends, in such cases, upon the philosopher. In spite of many misadventures, curiosity generally gets the better of caution.

He opens Comte's "Positive Philosophy" and reads, "In order to understand the true value and character of the 'Positive Philosophy' we must take a brief, general view of the progressive course of the human mind regarded as a whole." Then he is conducted through the three stages of the theological or fictitious, the metaphysical or abstract, and the scientific or positive; which last circle proves large enough only for Comte's own opinions. He is caught in a trap and goes round and round without finding the hole through which he came in.

" When a learned person asks one," says the
Gentle Reader, " to accompany him on a brief
general survey of the progressive course of the
human mind, regarded as a whole, I am apt to
be wary.  I want to know what he is up to.  I
fear the philosopher bearing historical gifts."

Yet where the trap is made of slighter fabric,
and he feels that he can break through at will, he
enjoys watching the author and his work.  How
marvelous are the powers of the human mind !
How the facts of experience can be bent to a
sternly logical formula !  And how the whole
trend of things seems to yield to an imperious
will that is stronger than fate !

Here is a book published in Wheeling, Virginia,
in 1809.  It is " A Narrative of the Introduction
and Progress of Christianity in Scotland, before
the Reformation ; and the Progress of Religion
since in Scotland and America."  We are told
that the history was read paragraph by paragraph
at a meeting of the Reformed Dissenting Presbytery at the Three Ridge Meeting House, and
unanimously approved.  At the beginning we are
taken into a wide place and given a comprehen-
sive view of early Christianity.  Then we are

shown how in the sixteenth century began a series
of godly reformations.    Christianity, bursting
through the barriers of Popery, began its resistless
flow toward the pure theology of the Three Ridge
Meeting House.    As the articles of the true faith
were increased the number of persons who were
able to hold correct opinions upon them all dimin-
ished.    The history, by perfectly logical processes, brings us down to the year 1799, when
secession had done its perfect work and the true
church had attained to an apostolic purity of doctrine and a more than apostolic paucity of mem-
bership.    It is with a fearful joy that the
historians proclaim the culmination of the age-
long evolution.    "O! the times we live in!    There
were but two of us to defend the doctrine of the
Bible and the Westminster Confession."    At the
time the history of the Progress of Christianity
was written there were but two ministers who held
the uncorrupted faith; namely, Robert Warwick
and Alexander McCoy.    These two brethren were
the joint authors of the history, and in their
capacity as church council gave it ecumenical
authority.    Had McCoy disagreed with Warwick
about Preterition, or had Warwick suspected

McCoy of Sublapsarianism, then we should have had two histories of Christianity instead of one. It would have appeared that all the previous developments of Christianity were significant only as preparing for the Great Schism.

" There is a great deal of this Three Ridge Meeting House kind of history," says the Gentle Reader, " and I confess I find it very instructive. I like to find out what the writers think on the questions of the day."

The fact is that there is a great deal of human nature even in learned people, and they cannot escape from the spell of the present moment. They are like the rest of us, and feel that they are living at the terminus of the road and not at a way station. The cynical reflection on the way in which the decisions of the Supreme Court follow the election returns suggests the way in which historical generalizations follow the latest telegraphic dispatches. Something happens and then we look up its historical antecedents. It seems as if everything had been pointing to this one event from the beginning.

" Here is a very readable History of Fans. The writer justly says that the subject is one that

has been much neglected. 'In England brief
sketches on the subject have occasionally appeared in the magazines, but thus far a History
of Fans has not been published in book form.
. . . The subject amply repays careful study, and
will not fail to interest the reader, provided the
demands on both his patience and his time are
not too great.' I confess that it is a line of research I have never taken up, but it is evident
that there is ample material. The beginning in-
spires confidence. 'The chain of tradition, followed as far as possible into the past, carries us
but to the time when the origin of the fan is derived from tradition.' It appears that we come
out upon firm ground when we reach the Maha-
bharata. But the question which arouses my
curiosity is, How did it occur to any one that
there should be a history of fans? The author
reveals the inciting cause, — 'The Loan Exhibition held at South Kensington in 1870 gave a
great impulse to the collection and decoration of
fans.' I suspect that almost all readable histories
have some such origin."

The title of Professor Freeman's " History of
Federal Government from the Foundation of the

Achaian League to the Disruption of the United States " was timely when the first volume was published in 1863. The terminal points seemed closely connected in 1862 and the spring of 1863. Gettysburg and Appomattox destroyed the line of communication. But there was a time when the subject had great dramatic unity.

One May morning the Gentle Reader saw in the newspapers the account of the victory of Admiral Dewey at Manila, and learned how the English people rejoiced over the success of American arms. " This will remake a great deal of history," he said, " and there will be a great revival of interest in Hengist and Horsa. These primitive Anglo-Saxon expansionists kept their own counsel, but it 's evident that the movement they set on foot must go on to its logical conclusion. When a competent scholar takes hold of the history it will be seen that it could n't stop with the Heptarchy or the destruction of the Spanish Armada. It was a foregone conclusion that these Anglo-Saxons would eventually take the Philippines."

When one by one the books began to come out he read them with eager interest. That there

should be histories of the triumphant progress of
Anglo-Saxondom, after the Spanish-American
war, he looked upon as something as inevitable
as the history of fans, after the South Kensington
Exhibition.   It was manifest destiny.

There is one page in the history books which
the Gentle Reader looks upon with a skeptical
smile ; it is that which contains the words, " The
End."

" The writer may think that the subject has
been exhausted, and that he has said the last
word ; but in reality there is no end."

He is well aware that at best he gets but a
glimpse of what is going on.   The makers of
history are for the most part unknown to the
writers of it.   He loves now and then to catch
sight of one of these unremembered multitudes.
For a moment the searchlight of history falls
upon him, and he stands blinking in the unaccus-
tomed glare, and then the light shifts and oblivion swallows him up.

He stops to meditate when he comes upon this
paragraph in Bishop Burnet's " History of his
Own Times."

" When King James I. was in Scotland he erected a new Bishopric, and made one Forbes Bishop.  He was a very learned and pious man; he had a strange faculty of preaching five or six hours at a time.  His way of life and devotion was thought monastic, and his learning lay in antiquity ; he studied to be a reconciler between Papists and Protestants, leaning rather to the first; he was a simple-hearted man and knew little of the world, so he fell into several errors of conduct, but died soon after suspected of Popery."

" That man Forbes," says the Gentle Reader, " does n't cut much of a figure on the pages of history.  Indeed, that is all that is said of him, yet I doubt not but that he was a much more influential man in his day than many of those bishops and reformers that I have been reading about. A learned man who has a faculty for preaching five or six hours at a time is a great conservative force.  He keeps things from going too fast. When one reads about the Reformation of the sixteenth century, one wonders that it did n't make a clean sweep.  We must remember the number of good Protestants who died suspected of Popery."

But though he loves to get a glimpse of Forbes and men of his kind, he knows that they are not of the stuff that readable histories are made of. The retarding influences of the times must be taken into account, but after all the historian is concerned with the people who are " in the van of circumstance." They may be few in number, but their achievements are the things worth telling.

" Every history," says the Gentle Reader, "should be a Book of Genesis. I want to see things in their beginnings and in their fresh growth. I do not care to follow the processes of decay. Fortunately there is no period when something is not beginning. 'Sweet is the genesis of things.' History is a perpetual springtime. New movements are always on foot. Even when I don't approve of them I want to know what they are like. When the band strikes up 'See the Conquering Hero come,' it 's sheer affectation not to look up. The conquering hero is always worth looking at, even if you do not approve of him. The historian who undertakes to tell what men at any period were about must be quick to detect their real enthusiasms. He

must join the victorious army and not cling to a
lost cause.   I have always thought that it was a
mistake for Gibbon to call his great work, 'The
History of the Decline and Fall of the Roman
Empire.'   The declining power of the Roman
Empire was not the great fact of those ten centuries.   There were powers which were not declining, but growing.   How many things were in
the making, — Christianity, Mohammedanism, the
new chivalry, the Germanic civilization.   As for
the Roman Empire, one could see that *that* game
was lost, and it was n't worth while to play it out
to the last move.   I could n't make those shadowy
Emperors at Constantinople seem like Cæsars —
and, for that matter, they were n't."

On this last point I think that the Gentle
Reader is correct, and that the great historian is
one who has a certain prophetic gift.   He is
quick to discern the signs of the times.   He
identifies himself so thoroughly with the age of
which he writes that he always seems to be at
the beginning of an era peering into the yet dim
future.   In this way he shares the hopes and
aspirations of the men of whom he writes.   For
there was a day when all our familiar institu-

tions were new.   There was a time when the
Papacy was not an established fact, but a vague
dream of spiritual power and unity, a challenge
to a barbarian world.   It appealed to young
idealists as the federation of the world or a
socialistic commonwealth appeals to-day.   There
was a time when constitutional government was
a Utopian experiment which a few brave men
were willing to try.   There was a time when
Calvinism was a spiritual adventure.

The historian whom we love is one who stands
at the parting of the ways, and sees ideals grow
into actualities.   He is not reminiscent.   He is
forward-looking as he speaks to each age out of
intimate acquaintance with its new hopes, as one

> " Who hath forsaken old and sacred thrones
>   For prophecies of thee, and for the sake
>   Of loveliness new born."

# The Evolution of the Gentleman

---

" WHAT is your favorite character, Gentle
Reader?" "I like to read about gentlemen," he answers; "it's a taste I have inher-
ited, and I find it growing upon me."

And yet it is not easy to define a gentleman, as
the multitudes who have made the attempt can
testify. It is one of the cases in which the dictionary does not help one. Perhaps, after all, definitions are to be looked upon as luxuries, not as
necessities. When Alice told her name to Humpty
Dumpty, that intolerable pedant asked, —

" ' What does it mean?'

" ' Must a name mean something?' Alice
asked doubtfully.

" ' Of course it must,' Humpty Dumpty said

with a short laugh. 'My name means the shape
I am, — and a good handsome shape it is, too.' "

I suppose that almost any man, if he were asked
what a gentleman is, would answer with Humpty
Dumpty, " It is the shape I am." I judge this
because, though the average man would not feel
insulted if you were to say, " You are no saint,"
it would not be safe to say, " You are no gentleman."

And yet the average man has his misgivings.
For all his confident talk, he is very humble
minded. The astral body of the gentleman that
he is endeavoring to project at his neighbors is
not sufficiently materialized for his own imperfect
vision. The word " gentleman " represents an
ideal. Above whatever coarseness and sordid-
ness there may be in actual life, there rises the
ideal of a finer kind of man, with gentler manners and truer speech and braver action.

In every age we shall find the true gentleman
— that is, the man who represents the best ideal
of his own time, and we shall find the mimicry
of him the would-be gentleman who copies the
form while ignorant of the substance. These
two characters furnish the material, on the one

hand for the romancer, and on the other for the
satirist.   If there had been no real gentlemen,
the epics, the solemn tragedies, and the stirring
tales of chivalry would have remained unwritten ;
and if there had been no pretended gentlemen,
the humorist would have lost many a pleasure.
Always the contrasted characters are on the stage
together ; simple dignity is followed by strutting
pomposity, and after the hero the braggart swag-
gers and storms.   So ridicule and admiration
bear rule by turns.

The idea of the gentleman involves the sense of
personal dignity and worth.   He is not a means
to an end ; he is an end in itself.   How early
this sense arose we may not know.   Professor
Huxley made merry over the sentimentalists who
picture the simple dignity of primitive man.   He
had no admiration to throw away on " the dignified and unclothed savage sitting in solitary medi-
tation under trees."   And yet I am inclined to
think that the gentleman must have appeared
even before the advent of tailors.   The peasants
who followed Wat Tyler sang, —

> " When Adam delved and Eve span
> Who was then the gentleman ? "

But a writer in the age of Queen Elizabeth published a book in which he argued that Adam himself was a perfect gentleman. He had the advantage, dear to the theological mind, that though affirmative proof might be lacking, it was equally difficult to prove the negative.

As civilization advances and literature catches its changing features, the outlines of the gentleman grow distinct.

In the Book of Genesis we see Abraham sitting at his tent door. Three strangers appear. When he sees them, he goes to meet them, and bows, and says to the foremost, " My Lord, if now I have found favour in thy sight, pass not away, I pray thee, from thy servant. Let a little water, I pray you, be fetched, and wash your feet, and rest yourselves under the tree : and I will fetch a morsel of bread, and comfort ye your hearts ; after that ye shall pass on."

There may have been giants in those days, and churls, and all manner of barbarians, but as we watch the strangers resting under the oak we say, "There were also gentlemen in those days." How simple it all is ! It is like a single palm tree outlined against the desert and the sky.

We turn to the Analects of Confucius and we see the Chinese gentleman.  Everything with him is exact.  The disciples of Confucius are careful to tell us how he adjusted the skirts of his robe before and behind, how he insisted that his mince-meat should be cut quite small and should have exactly the right proportion of rice, and that his mat must be laid straight before he would sit on it.  Such details of deportment were thought very important.  But we forget the mats and the mince-meat when we read: " Three things the master had not, — he had no prejudices, he had no obstinacy, he had no egotism."  And we forget the fantastic garb and the stiff Chinese genuflections, and come to the conclusion that the true gentleman is as simple-hearted amid the etiquette of the court as in the tent in the desert, when we hear the master saying: "Sincerity is the way of Heaven ; the wise are the unassuming.  It is said of Virtue that over her embroidered robe she puts a plain single garment."

When we wish to see a masculine virtue which has no need of an embroidered garment we go to Plutarch's portrait gallery of antique gentlemen.

What a breed of men they were! They were no
holiday gentlemen.   With the same lofty dignity
they faced life and death.   How superior they
were to their fortunes.   No wonder that men who
had learned to conquer themselves conquered the
world.

Most of Plutarch's worthies were gentlemen,
though there were exceptions.   There was, for
example, Cato the Censor, who bullied the Roman
youth into virtue, and got a statue erected to himself as the restorer of the good old manners.
Poor Plutarch, who likes to do well by his heroes,
is put to his wits' end to know what to do with
testy, patriotic, honest, fearless, parsimonious
Cato.   Cato was undoubtedly a great man and a
good citizen; but when we are told how he sold
his old slaves, at a bargain, when they became in-
firm, and how he left his war-horse in Spain to
save the cost of transportation, Plutarch adds,
" Whether such things be an evidence of greatness or littleness of soul let the reader judge for
himself."   The judicious reader will conclude
that it is possible to be a great man and a reformer, and yet not be quite a gentleman.

When the Roman Empire was destroyed the

antique type of gentleman perished.   The very
names of the tribes which destroyed him have yet
terrible associations.   Goths, Vandals, Huns — to
the civilized man of the fifth and sixth centuries
these sounded like the names of wild beasts rather
than of men.   You might as well have said tigers,
hyenas, wolves.   The end had come of a civilization that had been the slow growth of centuries.

Yet out of these fierce tribes, destroyers of the
old order, a new order was to arise.   Out of chaos
and night a new kind of gentleman was to be
evolved.   The romances of the Middle Ages are
variations on a single theme, the appearance of
the finer type of manhood and its struggle for
existence.   In the palace built by the enchantment of Merlin were four zones of sculpture.

> " And in the lowest beasts are slaying men,
>   And in the second men are slaying beasts,
>   And on the third are warriors, perfect men,
>   And on the fourth are men with growing wings."

Europe was in the second stage, when men were
slaying beasts and what was most brutal in humanity.   If the higher manhood was to live, it
must fight, and so the gentleman appears, sword
in hand.   Whether we are reading of Charle-

magne and his paladins, or of Siegfried, or of
Arthur, the story is the same. The gentleman
has appeared. He has come into a waste land,

> "Thick with wet woods and many a beast therein,
> And none or few to scare or chase the beast."

He comes amid savage anarchy where heathen
hordes are "reddening the sun with smoke and
earth with blood." The gentleman sends forth
his clear defiance. All this shall no longer be.
He is ready to meet force with force ; he is ready
to stake his life upon the issue, the hazard of new
fortunes for the race.

It is as a pioneer of the new civilization that
the gentleman has pitched

> "His tent beside the forest. And he drave
> The heathen, and he slew the beast, and felled
> The forest, and let in the sun."

The ballads and romances chronicle a struggle
desperate in its beginning and triumphant in its
conclusion. They are in praise of force, but it
is a noble force. There is something better, they
say, than brute force: it is manly force. The
giant is no match for the gentleman.

If we would get at the mediæval idea of the
gentleman, we must not listen merely to the

romances as they are retold by men of genius in
our own day.   Scott and Tennyson clothe their
characters in the old draperies, but their ideals
are those of the nineteenth century rather than of
the Middle Ages.   Tennyson expressly disclaims
the attempt to reproduce the King Arthur

> " whose name, a ghost,
> Streams like a cloud, man-shaped, from mountain peak,
> And cleaves to cairn and cromlech still ;  or him
> Of Geoffrey's book, or him of Malleor's, one
> Touched by the adulterous finger of a time
> That hovered between war and wantonness."

When we go back and read Sir Thomas Malory's
Morte Darthur, we find ourselves among men of
somewhat different mould from the knights of
Tennyson's idylls.   It is not the blameless King
Arthur, but the passionate Sir Launcelot, who
wins admiration.   We hear Sir Ector crying over
Launcelot's body, " Ah, Launcelot, thou wert the
head of the Christian knights.   Thou wert the
courtliest knight that ever bare shield ; and thou
wert the truest friend to thy lover that ever be-
strode horse ; and thou wert the truest lover for
a sinful man that ever loved woman ; and thou
wert the kindest man that ever strake with sword ;
and thou wert the goodliest person that ever came

among press of knights; and thou wert the meek-
est man and the gentlest that ever ate in hall with
ladies; and thou wert the sternest knight to thy
mortal foe that ever put spear in the rest."

We must take, not one of these qualities, but
all of them together, to understand the gentleman
of those ages when good and evil struggled so
fiercely for the mastery. No saint was this Sir
Launcelot. There was in him no fine balance of
virtues, but only a wild tumult of the blood. He
was proud, self-willed, passionate, pleasure-loving;
capable of great sin and of sublime expiation.
What shall we say of this gentlest, sternest, kindest, goodliest, sinfulest of knights, — this man
who knew no middle path, but who, when tread-
ing in perilous places and following false lights,
yet draws all men admiringly to himself?

We can only say this: he was the prototype of
those mighty men who were the makers of the
modern world. They were the men who fought
with Charlemagne, and with William the Con-
queror, and with Richard; they were the men
who "beat down the heathen, and upheld the
Christ;" they were the men from whom came
the crusades, and the feudal system, and the

great charter.   As we read the history, we say
at one moment, " These men were mail-clad
ruffians," and at the next, " What great-hearted
gentlemen ! "

Perhaps the wisest thing would be to confess
to both judgments at once.   In this stage of his
evolution the gentleman may boast of feats that
would now be rehearsed only in bar-rooms.   This
indicates that the standard of society has improved, and that what was possible once for the
nobler sort of men is now characteristic of the
baser sort.   The modern rowdy frequently appears in the cast-off manners of the old-time
gentleman.   Time, the old-clothes man, thus furnishes his customers with many strange misfits.
What is of importance is that through these
transition years there was a ceaseless struggle to
preserve the finer types of manhood.

The ideal of the mediæval gentleman was
expressed in the word " gallantry."   The essence
of gallantry is courage ; but it is not the sober
courage of the stoic.   It is courage charged with
qualities that give it sparkle and effervescence.
It is the courage that not only faces danger, but
delights in it.   What suggestions of physical and

mental elasticity are in Shakespeare's description
of the " springing, brave Plantagenet"! Scott's
lines express the gallant spirit: —

> "One crowded hour of glorious life
>    Is worth an age without a name."

Gallantry came to have another implication,
equally characteristic. The knight was gallant
not only in war, but in love also. There had
come a new worship, the worship of woman. In
the Church it found expression in the adoration
of the Madonna, but in the camp and the court
it found its place as well. Chivalry was the
elaborate and often fantastic ritual, and the gentleman was minister at the altar. The ancient
gentleman stood alone; the mediæval gentleman
offered all to the lady of his love. Here, too,
gallantry implied the same overflowing joy in
life. If you are anxious to have a test by which
to recognize the time when you are growing
old, — so old that imagination is chilled within
you, — I should advise you to turn to the chapter
in the Romance of King Arthur entitled " How
Queen Guenever went maying with certain
Knights of the Table Round, clad all in green."
Then read : " So it befell in the month of May,

Queen Guenever called unto her knights and she gave them warning that early upon the morrow she would ride maying into the woods and fields besides Westminster, and I warn you that none of you but that he be well horsed and that ye all be clothed in green. . . . I shall bring with me ten ladies and every knight shall have a squire and two yeomen. So upon the morn they took their horses with the Queen and rode on maying through the woods and meadows in great joy and delights."

If you cannot see them riding on, a gallant company over the meadows, and if you hear no echoes of their laughter, and if there is no longer any enchantment in the vision of that time when all were "blithe and debonair," then undoubtedly you are growing old. It is time to close the romances: perhaps you may still find solace in Young's "Night Thoughts" or Pollok's "Course of Time." Happy are they who far into the seventies still see Queen Guenever riding in the pleasant month of May: these are they who have found the true fountain of youth.

The gentleman militant will always be the hero of ballads and romances; and in spite of the apostles of realism, I fancy he has not lost his charm. There are Jeremiahs of evolution, who tell us that after a time men will be so highly developed as to have neither hair nor teeth. In that day, when the operating dentists have ceased from troubling, and given way to the manufacturing dentists, and the barbers have been superseded by the wig-makers, it is quite possible that the romances may give place to some tedious department of comparative mythology. In that day, Chaucer's knight who "loved chevalrie, trouthe and honour, fredom and curtesie," will be forgotten, though his armor on the museum walls will be learnedly described. But that dreadful day is still far distant; before it comes, not only teeth and hair must be improved out of existence, but a substitute must be found for good red blood. Till that time "no laggard in love or dastard in war" can steal our hearts from young Lochinvar.

The sixteenth century marks an epoch in the history of the gentleman, as in all else. Old ideas disappear, to come again in new combinations. Familiar words take on meanings that completely transform them. The same hands wielded the sword and the pen. The scholars, the artists, the poets, began to feel a sense of personal worth, and carried the gallant spirit of the gentleman into their work. They were not mere specialists, but men of action. The artist was not only an instrument to give pleasure to others, but he was himself a centre of admiration. Out of this new consciousness how many interesting characters were produced! There were men who engaged in controversies as if they were tournaments, and who wrote books and painted pictures and carved statues, not in the spirit of professionalism, but as those who would in this activity enjoy "one crowded hour of glorious life." Very frequently, these gentlemen and scholars, and gentlemen and artists, overdid the matter, and were more belligerent in disposition than were the warriors with whom they began to claim equality.

To this self-assertion we owe the most delightful of autobiographies, — that of Benvenuto Cellini. He aspired to be not only an artist, but a fine gentleman. No one could be more certain of the sufficiency of Humpty Dumpty's definition of a gentleman than was he.

If we did not have his word for it, we could scarcely believe that any one could be so valiant in fight and so uninterrupted in the pursuit of honor without its interfering with his professional work. Take, for example, that memorable day when, escaping from the magistrates, he makes an attack upon the household of his enemy, Gherardo Guascanti. " I found them at table; and Gherardo, who had been the cause of the quarrel, flung himself upon me. I stabbed him in the breast, piercing doublet and jerkin, but doing him not the least harm in the world." After this attack, and after magnanimously pardoning Gherardo's father, mother, and sisters, he says: " I ran storming down the staircase, and when I reached the street, I found all the rest of the household, more than twelve persons : one of them seized an iron shovel, another a thick iron pipe; one had an anvil, some hammers, some cudgels. When I got among them, raging like a mad bull, I flung four or five to the earth, and fell down with them myself, continually aiming my dagger now at one, and now at another. Those who remained upright plied with both hands with all their force, giving it me with hammers, cudgels, and the anvil; but inasmuch as God does sometimes mercifully intervene, he so ordered that neither they nor I did any harm to one another."

What fine old days those were, when the toughness of skin matched so wonderfully the stoutness of heart! One has a suspicion that in these degenerate times, were a family dinner-party interrupted by such an avalanche of daggers, cudgels, and anvils, some one would be hurt. As for Benvenuto, he does not so much as complain of a headache.

There is an easy, gentleman-like grace in the way in which he recounts his incidental homicides. When he is hiding behind a hedge at midnight, waiting for the opportunity to assassinate his enemies, his heart is open to all the sweet influences of nature, and he enjoys "the glorious heaven of stars." He was not only an artist and a fine gentleman, but a saint as well, and "often had recourse with pious heart to holy prayers." Above all, he had the indubitable evidence of sainthood, a halo. "I will not omit to relate another circumstance, which is perhaps the most remarkable that ever happened to any one. I do

so in order to justify the divinity of God and of
his secrets, who deigned to grant me this great
favor: forever since the time of my strange vision
until now, an aureole of glory (marvelous to relate) has rested on my head.  This is visible to
every sort of man to whom I have chosen to point
it out, but these have been few." He adds ingen-
uously, " I am always able to see it." He says,
" I first became aware of it in France, at Paris;
for the air in those parts is so much freer from
mists that one can see it far better than in Italy."

Happy Benvenuto with his Parisian halo,
which did not interfere with the manly arts of
self-defense! His self-complacency was possible
only in a stage of evolution when the saint and
the assassin were not altogether clearly differen-
tiated.  Some one has said, " Give me the luxuries of life, and I can get along without the
necessities." Like many of his time, Benvenuto
had all the luxuries that belong to the character
of a Christian gentleman, though he was destitute
of the necessities.  An appreciation of common
honesty as an essential to a gentleman seems to
be more slowly developed than the more romantic
sentiment that is called honor.

The evolution of the gentleman has its main line of progress where there is a constant though slow advance; but, on the other hand, there are arrested developments, and quaint survivals, and abortive attempts.

In each generation there have been men of fashion who have mistaken themselves for gentlemen. They are uninteresting enough while in the flesh, but after a generation or two they become very quaint and curious, when considered as specimens. Each generation imagines that it has discovered a new variety, and invents a name for it. The dude, the swell, the dandy, the fop, the spark, the macaroni, the blade, the popinjay, the coxcomb, — these are butterflies of different summers. There is here endless variation, but no advancement. One fashion comes after another, but we cannot call it better. One would like to see representatives of the different generations together in full dress. What variety in oaths and small talk! What anachronisms in swords and canes and eye-glasses, in ruffles, in collars, in wigs! What affluence in powders and perfumes and colors! But "will they know each other there"? The real gentlemen

would be sure to recognize each other. Abraham
and Marcus Aurelius and Confucius would find
much in common. Launcelot and Sir Philip
Sidney and Chinese Gordon would need no introduction. Montaigne and Mr. Spectator and
the Autocrat of the Breakfast-Table would fall
into delightful chat. But would a " swell "
recognize a " spark " ? And might we not expect a " dude " to fall into immoderate laughter
at the sight of a " popinjay " ?

Fashion has its revenges. Nothing seems so
ridiculous to it as an old fashion. The fop has
no toleration for the obsolete foppery. The
artificial gentleman is as inconceivable out of his
artificial surroundings as the waxen-faced gentleman of the clothing store outside his show
window.

There was Beau Nash, for example, — a much-
admired person in his day, when he ruled from
his throne in the pump-room in Bath. Everything was in keeping. There was Queen Anne
architecture, and Queen Anne furniture, and
Queen Anne religion, and the Queen Anne fashion in fine gentlemen. What a curious piece of
bricabrac this fine gentleman was, to be sure!

He was not fitted for any useful purpose under the sun, but in his place he was quite ornamental, and undoubtedly very expensive. Art was as self-complacent as if nature had never been invented. What multitudes of the baser sort must be employed in furnishing the fine gentleman with clothes! All Bath admired the way in which Beau Nash refused to pay for them. Once when a vulgar tradesman insisted on payment, Nash compromised by lending him twenty pounds, — which he did with the air of a prince. So great was the impression he made upon his time that a statue was erected to him, while beneath were placed the busts of two minor contemporaries, Pope and Newton. This led Lord Chesterfield to write: —

> " This statue placed the busts between
> Adds to the satire strength,
> Wisdom and wit are little seen,
> But folly at full length."

Lord Chesterfield himself had nothing in common with the absurd imitation gentlemen, and yet the gentleman whom he described and pretended to admire was altogether artificial. He was the Machiavelli of the fashionable world.

He saw through it, and recognized its hollowness; but such as it was it must be accepted. The only thing was to learn how to get on in it. "In courts you may expect to meet connections without friendships, enmities without hatred, honor without virtue, appearances saved and realities sacrificed, good manners and bad morals."

There is something earnestly didactic about Lord Chesterfield. He gives line upon line, and precept upon precept, to his "dear boy." Never did a Puritan father teach more conscientiously the shorter catechism than did he the whole duty of the gentleman, which was to save appearances even though he must sacrifice reality. "My dear boy," he writes affectionately, "I advise you to trust neither man nor woman more than is absolutely necessary. Accept proffered friendships with great civility, but with great incredulity."

No youth was more strenuously prodded up the steep and narrow path of virtue than was little Philip Stanhope up the steep and narrow path of fashion. Worldliness made into a religion was not without its asceticism. "Though you

think you dance well, do not think you dance
well enough.    Though you are told that you are
genteel, still aim at being genteeler. . . . Airs,
address, manners, graces, are of such infinite
importance and are so essentially necessary to
you that now, as the time of meeting draws near,
I tremble for fear that I may not find you possessed of them."

Lord Chesterfield's gentleman was a man of
the world ; but it was, after all, a very hard and
empty world.    It was a world that had no eternal
laws, only changing fashions.    It had no broken
hearts, only broken vows.    It was a world cov-
ered with glittering ice, and the gentleman was
one who had learned to skim over its dangerous
places, not caring what happened to those who
followed him.

It is a relief to get away from such a world,
and, leaving the fine gentleman behind, to take
the rumbling stagecoach to the estates of Sir
Roger de Coverley.    His is not the great world
at all, and his interests are limited to his own
parish.    But it is a real world, and much better
suited to a real gentleman.    His fashions are
not the fashions of the court, but they are the

fashions that wear. Even when following the hounds Sir Roger has time for friendly greetings. " The farmers' sons thought themselves happy if they could open a gate for the good old knight, which he requited with a nod or a smile, and a kind inquiry after their fathers and uncles."

But even dear old Roger de Coverley cannot rest undisturbed as an ideal gentleman. He belonged, after all, to a privileged order, and there is a force at work to destroy all social privileges. A generation of farmers' sons must arise not to be so easily satisfied with a kindly nod and smile. Liberty, fraternity, and equality have to be reckoned with. Democracy has come with its leveling processes.

> " The calm Olympian height
> Of ancient order feels its bases yield."

In a revolutionary period the virtues of an aristocracy become more irritating than their vices. People cease to attribute merit to what comes through good fortune. No wonder that the disciples of the older time cry : —

> " What hope for the fine-nerved humanities
> That made earth gracious once with gentler arts ? "

What becomes of the gentleman in an age of democratic equality?  Just what becomes of every ideal when the time for its fulfillment has come.  It is freed from its limitations and enters into a larger life.

Let us remember that the gentleman was always a lover of equality, and of the graces that can only grow in the society of equals.  The gentleman of an aristocracy is at his best only when he is among his peers.  There is a little circle within which there is no pushing, no assumption of superiority.  Each member seeks not his own, but finds pleasure in a gracious interchange of services.

But an aristocracy leaves only a restricted sphere for such good manners.  Outside the group to which he belongs the gentleman is compelled by imperious custom to play the part of a superior being.  It has always been distasteful and humiliating to him.  It is only an essentially vulgar nature that can really be pleased with the servility of others.

An ideal democracy is a society in which good manners are universal.  There is no arrogance and no cringing, but social intercourse is based on mutual respect. This ideal democracy has not been perfected, but the type of men who are creating it has already been evolved. Among all the crude and sordid elements of modern life, we see the stirring of a new chivalry. It is based on a recognition of the worth and dignity of the common man.

Milton in memorable words points out the transition which must take place from the gentleman of romance to the gentleman of enduring reality. After narrating how, in his youth, he betook himself "to those lofty fables and romances which recount in solemn cantos the deeds of knighthood founded by our victorious kings and thence had in renown through all Christendom," he says, "This my mind gave me that every free and gentle spirit, without that oath ought to be born a knight, nor needed to expect a gilt spur or the laying on of a sword upon his shoulder."

# The Hinter-land of Science

❧

A GENIAL critic detects a note of exaggeration in my praise of Ignorance. It is, he declares, a bit of "Yellow Journalism." The reader's attention is attracted by a glaring headline which leads him to suppose that a crime has been committed, when in reality nothing out of the ordinary has happened. That a person who has emerged from the state of absolute illiteracy far enough to appear in print should express a preference for Ignorance would be important if true. After perusing the chapter, however, he is of the opinion that it is not Ignorance, at all, that is described, but something much more respectable. It is akin to a state of mind which literary persons have agreed to praise under the name of Culture.

It is very natural that these literary persons should prefer a high-sounding name, and one free from vulgar associations, but I do not think that their plea will stand the test of scientific analysis. Science will not tolerate half knowledge nor pleasant imaginings, nor sympathetic appreciations ; it must have definite demonstration. The knowledge of the best that has been said and thought may be very consoling, but it implies an unscientific principle of selection. It can be proved by statistics that the best things are exceptional. What about the second best, not to speak of the tenth rate ? It is only when you have collected a vast number of commonplace facts that you are on the road to a true generalization.

In the Smithsonian Institution at Washington there is a children's room, in which there is a case marked " Pretty Shells." The specimens fully justify the inscription. The very daintiest shapes, and the most intricate convolutions, and the most delicate tints are represented. They are pretty shells, which have not left their beauty on the shore. But the delight in all this loveliness is not scientific. The kind gentleman who arranged the shells according to this classification acted not in his capacity as a conchologist, but as the father of a family.

Nor does the enjoyment of the most beautiful thoughts or words satisfy the requirements of those sciences which deal with humanity. The distinction between Literature and Science is fundamental. What is a virtue in one sphere is a vice in the other. After all that has been said about the scientific use of the imagination it remains true that the imagination is an intruder in the laboratory. Even if it were put to use, that would only mean that it is reduced to a condition of slavery. In its own realm it is accustomed to play rather than to work. It is also true that the attempts to introduce the methods of the laboratory into literature have been dismal failures. That way dullness lies.

Now and then, indeed, Nature in a fit of prodigality endows one person with both gifts. — Was not Oliver Wendell Holmes a Professor of Anatomy? In such a case there is a perpetual effervescence. But even Dr. Holmes could not insinuate a sufficient knowledge of Anatomy by means of a series of discursive essays; nor could

he give scientific value to the reflections of the
" Autocrat of the Breakfast Table."

There was a time when the ability to read was
such a rare accomplishment that it seemed to
furnish the key to all knowledge. Men of the
baser sort had to learn by experience, but the
reader followed a royal path to the very fountain
head of wisdom. Ordinary rules were not for
him ; he could claim the benefit of clergy. Only
a generation ago young men of parts prepared
themselves for the bar — and very good lawyers
they made — by " reading Blackstone." Blackstone is a pleasant author, with a fund of wise
observations, and many pleasant afternoons were
spent in his company. In like manner other
young men " read medicine."

It is now coming to be understood that one
cannot read a science ; it must be studied in quite
a different fashion. " Book-learning " in such
matters has been discredited.

The Gentle Reader has learned this lesson. It
may be that he has cultivated some tiny field of
his own, and has thus come to know how different
this laborious task is from the care-free wandering in which at other hours he delights. But

though he cannot read his way into the domains
of strict science, yet there is an adjacent territory
which he frequents. Into this territory, though
he holds an ambiguous position, and finds many
to molest and make him afraid, he is drawn by
an insatiable curiosity. In a border-land danger
has attractions and mystery is alluring. There
is pleasant reading in spite of many threatening
technicalities which seem to bar further progress.

On the coasts of the Dark Continent of Ignorance the several sciences have gained a foothold.
In each case there is a well-defined country carefully surveyed and guarded. Within its frontiers
the laws are obeyed, and all affairs are carried
on in an orderly fashion. Beyond it is a vague
"sphere of influence," a Hinter-land over which
ambitious claims of suzerainty are made ; but the
native tribes have not yet been exterminated, and
life goes on very much as in the olden time. Into
the Hinter-land the Gentle Reader wanders, and
he is known to the scientific explorer as a friendly
native, whose good-will is worth cultivating. He
is often confounded with the "General Reader,"
a very different person, whose omnivorous appetite and intemperance in the use of miscellaneous

information are very offensive to him.  Unscrupulous adventurers carry on a thriving trade with
the General Reader in damaged goods, which are
foisted on him under the name of Popular Science.

In the Hinter-land there is dense ignorance of
the achievements and even of the names of most
of those who are recognized as authorities in their
several sciences.  They are as unknown as is the
Lord Mayor of London to the natives on the
banks of the Zambesi.  The heroes of the Hinter-land are the bold explorers who in militant
fashion have made their way into regions as yet
unsubdued.

In the middle of the nineteenth century there
was an heroic period during which scientific in-
vestigation took on all the color of romance.
The Gentle Reader turns to the lives and works
of Darwin, Huxley, and Tyndall, very much as
he would turn to the tales of Charlemagne and
his Paladins.  Here was a field of action.  Something happened.  As he reads he is conscious
that he has nothing of that impersonal attitude
which belongs to pure science.  It is not scientific but human interest which moves him.  He

is anxious to know what these men did, and what was the result of their deeds. It is an intellectual adventure of which the outcome is still uncertain.

The new generation cannot fully realize what the word " Evolution " meant to those who saw in it a portent of mysterious change. In its early advocates there was a mingling of romantic daring and missionary zeal. Its enemies resisted with the fortitude which belongs to those who never know when they are beaten. In almost any old bookstores one may see a counter labeled "Second-hand Theology, very cheap." It is a collection of the spent ammunition which may still be found on the field of battle. It is in an unfrequented corner. Now and then a theological student may visit it, but even he seems rather to be a vague considerer of worthy things than a bargain hunter. Yet once these volumes were eagerly read.

Out of the border warfare between Science and certain types of Theology and Philosophy there came a kind of literature that has a very real value and which is not lacking in charm. What a sense of relief came to the Gentle Reader when he stumbled upon John Fiske's " Excursions of an Evolutionist." This was the very thing he had been looking for ; not an exhaustive survey, nor a strenuous campaign, but an excursion with a competent guide and interpreter, a friendly person acquainted with the country who would tell him the things he wanted to know, and not weary him with irrelevant and confusing details.

What an admirable interpreter Fiske was! Darwin, with characteristic modesty, acknowledged his indebtedness to him for pointing out some of the larger results of his own investigations. He had the instinct which enabled him to seize the salient points ; to open up new vistas, to make clear a situation. His histories are always readable because he followed the main stream and never lost himself in a sluggish bayou. The same method applied to cosmic forces makes him see their dramatic movement. It is the genius of a born man of letters using the facts discovered by scientific methods for its own purpose. That purpose is always broad and humanizing.

The specialist is apt to speak patronizingly of such work, as if it were necessarily inferior to his own. It seems to bear the marks of superficial-

ity.  To appreciate it properly one must take it
for what it is.  Man was interested in the Universe long before he began to study it scientifi-
cally.  He dreamed about it, he mused over its
mysteries, he talked about its more obvious as-
pects.  And it is as interesting now as it ever
was and as fit an object of thought.  The con-
ceptions which satisfied us in the days when ignorance had not arrived at self-consciousness have
to be given up; but we are anxious to know what
have taken their places.  We want to get our
bearings and to discern the general trend of the
forces which make the world.  It is no mean
order of mind that is fitted to answer our needs
by wise interpretation.

There is often a conflict between private own-
ers and the public over the right to fish in certain
waters.  The landowners put up warning signs
and try to prevent trespass, while the public insists on its ancient privileges.  The law, with
that admirable common sense for which it has
such a great reputation, makes a distinction.
The small pond may be privately owned and
fenced in, but " boatable waters " are free to all.

So we may concede to the specialist the exclu-

sive right to have an opinion on certain subjects — subjects let us say of a size suitable for
the thesis of a Doctor of Philosophy.   But we
are not to be shut off from the pleasure of thinking on more sizable themes.   We have all equal
rights on the "boatable waters."

Matthew Arnold retells the story of the Scho-
lar-gypsy who, forsaking the university, " took to
the woods," — so far as we can learn from the
poem, to his own spiritual and intellectual advantage.   The combination of the scholar and
gypsy has a fascination.   One likes to conceive of
thought as playing freely among the other forces
of nature, and dealing directly with all objects
and not with those especially prepared for it.

Across the border-land of the physical sciences
one may meet many such scholar-gypsies.   They
have taken to the wilderness and yet carried into
it a trained intelligence.   Here may be found
keen observers, who might have written text-books
on ornithology had they not fallen in love with
birds.   They follow their friends into their haunts
in the thickets, and they love to gossip about their
peculiarities.   Here are botanists who love the

growing things in the fields and woods better
than the specimens in their herbariums. They
love to describe better than to analyze. Now and
then one may meet a renegade who carries a geo-
logist's hammer. It is a sheer hypocrisy, like a
fishing rod in the hands of a contemplative ram-
bler. It is merely an excuse for being out of
doors and among the mountains.

The Gentle Reader finds unfailing delight in
these wanderers. They open up to him a leafy
world. Thanks to them there are places where
he feels intimately at home: a certain English
parish; a strip of woodland in Massachusetts;
the vicinity of a farm on the Hudson; an enchanted country in the high Sierras.

"I verily believe," he says, "there is more
Natural History to be learned in such places than
in all the museums. Besides, I never liked a
museum."

The fact is that he does learn a good many
things in this way — and some of them he remembers.

The native African who is capable of understanding the philosophy of history may adjust

his mind to the idea that his continent is intended
for exploitation by a superior race.    The forests
in which his ancestors have hunted for generations form only a part of the Hinter-land of some
colony on the coast which he has never seen.
After a time, by an inevitable process of expansion, the colony will absorb and assimilate all the
adjoining country.    But his perplexities are not
over when he has, in a general way, resigned
himself to manifest destiny.    He discovers that
all Europeans are not alike, though they certainly
look alike.    There are conflicting claims.    To
whose sphere of influence does he belong?    It is
not easy to answer such questions, and mistakes
are liable to bring down upon him punitive ex-
peditions from different quarters.

A similar perplexity arises in the minds of
the simple inhabitants of the scientific Hinter-
lands.    They are ready to admit the superior
claims of the exact sciences, but they are puz-
zled to know to what particular sphere they belong.

In the absence of any generally received philosophy each special science pushes out as far as
it can and attempts to take in the whole of exist-

ence.   The specialist, forgetting his self-imposed
limitations, and fired with the ambition for wide
generalization, which is the infirmity of all active
minds, becomes an intellectual tyrant.   He is a
veritable Tamerlane, and if he rears no pyramids
of skulls, he leaves behind him a multitude of
muddled brains.

Wilberforce tells us of the havoc wrought in
his day by the new science of Political Economy.
Adam Smith's " Wealth of Nations " was hailed
as the complete solution of all social problems.
Forgetting the narrow scope of the inquiry which
had to do with only a single aspect of human
life, the maxims of trade were elevated into the
place of the moral law.   Superstition magnified
those useful twins, Demand and Supply, into
two all-powerful Genii who were quite capable of
doing the work of Providence.   For any one in
the spirit of brotherly kindness to interfere with
their autocratic operations was looked upon as
an act of rebellion against the nature of things.
" A dismal science," indeed, as any science is
when it becomes an unlimited despotism.

At the present time Geology is a very modest
science, remaining peacefully within its natural

frontiers; but in the days of Hugh Miller it was viewed with alarm. Elated with its victory in the affair with Genesis, its adherents were filled with militant ardor and were in the mood for universal conquest. In alliance with Chemistry it invaded the sphere of morals. Was not even Ruskin induced to write of the " Ethics of the Dust "? In the form of Physical Geography and with the auxiliary forces of Meteorology, it was ready to recast human history. Books were written to show that all civilization could be sufficiently explained by one who took account only of such features of the world as soil and climate.

While learned men were geologizing through the successive stratifications of humanity, a new claimant appeared. Biology became easily the paramount power. Its fame spread far and wide among those who knew nothing of its severer methods. In the Hinter-land the worship of Protoplasm became a cult. The hopes and fears and spiritual powers of humanity seemed illusory unless such phenomena were confirmed by analogies drawn from " the psychic life of micro-organisms." Fortunately at about this time the aggressive temper of "The New Psychology" did much to restore the balance of power. Under its influence those who still adhered to the belief that the proper study of mankind is man took heart and ventured, though with caution, to move abroad. The new Psychology in its turn has developed imperialistic ambitions. Its conquests have not been without much devastation, especially in the fair fields of education. A distinguished Psychologist has sounded a note of warning. He would have psychological experiments confined to the laboratory, leaving the school - room to the wholesome government of common sense. It is doubtful, however, whether such protests will avail any more than the eloquence of the Little Englanders has been able to limit colonial expansion.

The border-land between Psychology and Sociology is the scene of many a foray. The Psychologist thinks nothing of following a fleeing idea across the frontier. He deals confidently with the "Psychology of the mob," and "the aggregate mind," and the hypnotic influence of the crowd. There is such an air of authority about it all, that we forget that he is dealing with figures of speech.    On the other hand, the Sociologist attempts to solve the most delicate problems of the individual soul by the statistical method.

The Hinter-land has not yet been reduced to order.    The Gentle Reader suspects that no one of the rival sciences is strong enough to impose its own laws over so wide a region.    Perhaps, after all, they may have to call upon Philosophy to undertake the task of forming a responsible government.

# The Gentle Reader's Friends among the Clergy

$\prec\!\!\sim\!\!\succ$

"THERE has been a sad falling off in clerical character," says the Gentle Reader. "In the old books it is a pleasure to meet a parson. He is so simple and hearty that you feel at home with him at once. You know just where to find him, and he always takes himself and his profession for granted. He may be a trifle narrow, but you make allowance for that, and as for his charity it has no limits. You expect him to give away everything he can lay hands on. As for his creed it is always the same as the church to which he belongs, which is a great relief and saves no end of trouble. But the clergyman I meet with in novels nowadays is in a chronic

state of fidgetiness.   Nothing is as it seems or
as it ought to be.   He is as full of problems as
an egg is full of meat.   Everything resolves
itself into a conflict of duties, and whichever
duty he does he wishes it had been the other one.
When the poor man is not fretting because of
evil-doers he begins to fret because of the well-
doers, who do well in the old fashion without
any proper knowledge of the Higher Criticism or
Sanitary Drainage.   What with his creed and his
congregation and his love affairs, all of which
need mending, he lives a distracted life.   Though
the author in the first chapter praises his athletic
prowess, he seems to have no staying powers and
his nerves give out under the least strain.   He
is one of those trying characters of whom some
one has said that 'we can hear their souls
scrape.'   I prefer the old-time parsons.   They
were much more comfortable and in more rugged
health.   I like the phrase 'Bishops and other
Clergy.'   The bishops are great personages
whose lives are written like the lives of the Lord
Chancellors ; and they are not always very
readable.   But my heart goes out to the other
clergy, the good sensible men who were neither

great scholars nor reformers nor martyrs, and
who therefore did not get into the Church Histories, but who kept things going."

When he turns to the parson of " The Canterbury Tales" he finds the refreshment that comes
from contact with a perfectly wholesome nature.
Here is an enduring type of natural piety. In
the person of the good man the prayers of the
church for the healthful spirit of grace had been
answered in full measure. In his ministry in his
wide parish we cannot imagine him as being
worried or hurried. There could be for him no
conflict of duties; the duties plodded along one
after another in sturdy English fashion. And
when the duties were well done that was the end
of them. Their pale uneasy ghosts did not disturb his slumbers, and point with vague menace
to the unattainable. The parson had his place
and his definite task. He trod the earth as firmly
and sometimes as heavily as did the ploughman.

If the virtues of the fourteenth-century parson
were of the enduring order, so were his foibles.
The Gentle Reader is familiar with his weaknesses; for has he not " sat under his preaching?" The homiletic habit is hard to break, and

renders its victim strangely oblivious to the passage of time.    Every incident suggests a text
and every text suggests a new application.    In
the homiletic sphere perpetual motion is an
assured success.

What sinking of heart must have come to lay-
men like the merchant and the yeoman when the
parson on the pleasant road to Canterbury called
their attention to the resemblance between their
journey and

> " . . . thilke parfit, glorious pilgrymage,
>      That highte Jerusalem celestial."

They knew the symptoms.    When the homilist
has got scent of an analogy he will run it down,
however long the chase.

It would be interesting to discover the origin
of the impression so persistent in the lay mind
that sermons are long.    A sermon is seldom as
long as it seems.    But it is always with trepida-
tion that the listener observes in a discourse a
constitutional tendency to longevity.    In his
opinion the good die young.    As it is to-day so
it was on the afternoon when the host, with ill-
concealed alarm, called upon the good parson to
take his turn.

"Telleth," quod he, " youre meditacioun ;
But hasteth yow, the sonne wole adoun.
Beth fructuous, and that in litel space."

It is needless to say that what the parson called
his " little tale in prose" proved to be one of his
old sermons which he delivered without notes.
He was very unskillful in concealing his text,
which was Jeremiah vi. 16.

We are familiar with that interesting picture
of the pilgrims as they set out in the morning,
each figure alert.  I wonder that some one has
not painted a picture of them about sunset, as
the parson was in the middle of his discourse.
It is said that in every battle there is a critical
moment when each side is almost exhausted.
The side which at this moment receives rein-
forcements or rallies for a supreme effort gains
the victory.  So one must have noticed in every
over-long discourse a critical moment when the
speaker and his hearers are equally exhausted.
If at that moment the speaker, who has apparently used up his material, boldly announces
a new head, the hearers' discomfiture is complete.
This point of strategy the parson, guileless as he
was, understood and so managed to get in the

last word, so that "The Canterbury Tales" end
with the Canterbury sermon.

By the way, there was one ministerial weakness from which Chaucer's parson was free,—
the love of alliteration.  One is often struck,
when listening to a fervent discourse against
besetting sins, with the curious fact that all the
transgressions begin with the same letter of the
alphabet.  There is something suspicious in this
circumstance.  Not a great many years ago a
political party suffered severely because its candidate received an address from a worthy clergyman who was addicted to this habit, and instead
of the usual three R's enumerated "Rum, Roman-
ism, and Rebellion."  The chances are that he
meant no offense to his Roman Catholic fellow
citizens; but once on the toboggan slide of alliteration he could not stop.  If instead of rum he had
begun with whiskey, his homiletic instinct would
have led him to assert that the three perils of the
Republic were whiskey, war, and woman-suffrage.

It is to the credit of Chaucer's parson that
he distinctly repudiated alliteration with all its
allurements, especially in connection with the
seductive letter R.

"I kan nat geeste '*rum, ram, ruf,*' by lettre;
Ne, God woot, rym holde I but litel bettre."

When it came to plain prose without any rhetori-
cal embellishments, he was in his element.

It must be confessed that the clergyman is
not an eminently Shakespearean character.  The
great high ecclesiastics, like Pandulph and Wol-
sey, are great personages who make a fine show,
but the other clergy are not always in good and
regular standing.  They are sometimes little
better than hedge-priests.  But what pleasant
glimpses we get into the unwritten history of the
English Church in the days when it was still
Merry England.  The Cranmers and the Ridleys
made a great stir in those days, but no rumors of
it reached the rural parishes where Holofernes
kept school and Nathanael warmed over for his
slumbering congregation the scraps he had stolen
in his youth from the feast of the languages.  As
for the parishioners, they were doubtless well satisfied and could speak after the fashion of Con-
stable Dull when he was reproved for his silence.

"Goodman Dull, thou hast said no word all
this while."

Dull, — "Nor understood none neither, sir!"

The innocent pedant whose learning lies in the dead languages and who has a contempt for the living world is a type not extinct; but what shall we say of the Welsh curate of Windsor, Hugh Evans? In Windsor Park Mrs. Ford whispers, "Where is Nan now and her troop of fairies, and that Welsh devil Sir Hugh?"

That was her affectionate, though not respectful, way of referring to her spiritual adviser. Curate Evans was certainly not an example of what has been termed "the mild and temperate spirituality which has always characterized the Church of England." The dignity of the cloth is not in his mind as he cries, "Trib, fairies, trib, come and remember your parts, pe pold, I pray you, ... when I give the watch'ords do as I pid you."

Yet though he seemed not to put so much emphasis on character in religion as we in these more serious days think fitting, this Welsh devil of a parson had enough of the professional spirit to wish to point a moral on all proper occasions. Not too obtrusive or moral, nor carrying it to the sweating point, but a good, sound approbation of right sentiment. When Master Slender declares his resolution, " After this trick I 'll ne'er be drunk while I live again but in honest, civil, godly company. If I be drunk I 'll be drunk with those who fear God," the convivial curate responds, " So God judge me that shows a virtuous mind."

That Shakespeare intended any reflection on the Welsh clergy is not probable ; but so late as the eighteenth century a traveler in Wales remarks that the ale house was usually kept by the parson. One wonders whether with such manifest advantages the Welsh ministers' meetings were given over to lugubrious essays on " Why we do not reach the masses."

Shakespeare uses the word Puritan once, but Malvolio was a prig rather than a true Puritan. His objection to cakes and ale was rather because revelry disturbed his slumbers than because it troubled his conscience. But when we turn to Ben Jonson's Alchemist and come across Tribulation Wholesome, from Amsterdam, we know that the battle between the stage and the conventicle has begun. We know the solid virtues of these sectaries from whom came some of the best things in England and New England. But we must not expect to find this side of their character in the literature of the next two or three centuries. Unfortunately the non-conformist conscience was offended at those innocent pleasures in which amiable writers and readers have always taken satisfaction.

Charles Lamb inclined to the opinion of his friend who held that " a man cannot have a good conscience who refuses apple dumpling." The gastronomic argument against Puritanism has always been a strong one with the English mind. It was felt that a person must be a hypocrite who could speak disrespectfully of the creature comforts. There was no toleration for the miserable pretender who would " blaspheme custard through the nose." Tribulation Wholesome was deserving only of the pillory. There was no doubt but that the viands which were publicly reprobated were privately enjoyed.

> " You rail against plays to please the alderman
>   Whose daily custard you devour.
>   . . . You call yourselves
>   By names of Tribulation, Persecution,
>   Restraint, Long Patience and such-like, affected
>   Only for glory and to catch the ear
>   Of the disciple."

In "Bartholomew Fair" we meet Mr. Zeal of the Land Busy, an unlicensed exhorter, who has attained the liberty of prophesying, and is the leader of a little flock.

Did history keep on repeating itself, or did literary men keep on repeating each other? At any rate Mr. Zeal of the Land Busy reappears continually. He is in every particular the proto-type of those painful brethren who roused the wrath of honest Sam Weller. We recognize his unctuous speech, his unfailing appetite, and even his offensive and defensive alliance with the mother-in-law.

Mr. Little-Wit introduces him as "An old elder from Banbury who puts in here at meal times to praise the painful brethren and to pray that the sweet singers may be restored ; and he says grace as long as his breath lasts."

To which Mrs. Little-Wit responds, "Yes, indeed, we have such a tedious time with him, what for his diet and his clothes too, he breaks his buttons and cracks seams at every saying that he sobs out."

In answer to the anxious inquiry of his mother-in-law, Dame Pure-Craft, Little-Wit announces

that he has found the good man "with his teeth
fast in the cold turkey-pie in the cupboard, with
a great white loaf on his left hand, and a glass
of malmsey on his right." In Dame Pure-Craft
he finds a stanch supporter. "Slander not the
brethren, wicked one," she cries.

Zeal of the Land Busy attempts to lead his flock
through the perils of Bartholomew Fair. "Walk
in the middle of the way — turn neither to the
right nor to the left. Let not your eyes be drawn
aside by vanity nor your ears by noises." It was
indeed a dangerous journey, for it was nothing
less than "a grove of hobby horses and trinkets;
the wares are the wares of devils, and the fair is
the shop of Satan."

But, alas, though the eyes and ears were
guarded, another avenue of temptation had been
forgotten. The delicious odor of roast pig came
from one of the booths. It was a delicate little
pig, cooked with fire of juniper and rosemary
branches. Mrs. Little-Wit longed for it and her
husband encouraged her weakness. Dame Pure-
Craft rebukes him and bids him remember the
wholesome admonition of their leader.

Zeal of the Land Busy is a casuist of no mean

ability, and is equal to the task of finding an exception to his own rule.

" It may offer itself by other means to the sense, as by way of steam, which I think it doth in this place, huh! huh!—yes, it doth. And it were a sin of obstinacy, high and horrible obstinacy, to resist the titillation of the famelic sense which is smell. Therefore be bold, follow the scent; enter the tents of the unclean for this once, and satisfy your wife's frailty. Let your frail wife be satisfied; your zealous mother and my suffering self will be satisfied also."

Zeal of the Land Busy was like a certain English statesman of whom it was said, " His conscience, instead of being his monitor, became his accomplice."

One characteristic of these unlicensed exhorters seems to be very persistent, — their almost superhuman fluency. Despising preparation and trusting to the inspiration of the moment, they are never left without words. Preaching without notes is not particularly difficult if one has something to say, but these exhorters attempt to preach without notes and also without ideas. They require nothing but a word to begin with.

The speaker is like an army which, having broken away from its base of supplies, lives on the country through which it is marching. The hortatory guerrilla gets forage enough in one sentence to carry him on through the next. This was the homiletical method which Zeal of the Land used in his discourse at the fair. At a venture he cries out, —

"Down with Dagon!"

Leather-Head, the hobby-horse seller, asks very imprudently, —

"What do you mean, sir!"

That was enough; a torrent of impromptu eloquence is let loose.

"I will remove Dagon there, I say; that idol, that heathenish idol, that remains as I may say a beam, a very beam, not a beam of the sun, nor a beam of the moon, nor a beam of the balance, neither a house beam, nor a weaver's beam, but a beam in the eye, an exceeding great beam!"

It was the same method employed long after by Mr. Chadband in his moving address to little Joe.

"My young friend, you are to us a pearl, a diamond, you are to us a jewel. And why, my young friend?"

"I don't know," replied Joe, "I don't know nothink."

This gave Mr. Chadband his opportunity for continued speech. "My young friend, it is because you know nothing that you are to us a gem, a jewel. For what are you? Are you a beast of the field? No! Are you a fish of the river? No! You are a human boy! Oh, glorious to be a human boy! And why glorious, my young friend?"

Marvelous, to taciturn folk, is this flow of language. The little rill becomes a torrent, and soon there are waters to swim in. It seems to savor of the supernatural, being of the nature of creation out of nothing. And yet like many other wonderful things, it is easy when one knows how to do it.

The churchmen of those days joined with the wits in laughter which greeted the tinkers and the bakers who turned to prophesying on their own account. But now and then one of the zealous independents could give as keen a thrust as any which were received. It would be hard to find more delicate satire than in the description of Par-

son Two Tongues of the town of Fair Speech, who
was much esteemed by his distinguished parishioners, My Lord Time-Server, Mr. Facing Both-
Ways, and Mr. Anything.  The parson was a man
of good family, though his grandfather had been
a waterman, and had thus learned the art of looking one way and rowing another.  It is his parishioner Mr. Bye-Ends who propounds the question of ministerial ethics.  " Suppose a minister, a
worthy man, possessed of but a small benefice,
has in his eye a greater, more fat and plump by
far ; he has also now an opportunity of getting
it, yet so as being more studious, by preaching
more zealously, and because the temper of the
people requires it, by altering some of his principles, for my part I see no reason but a man may
do this (provided he has a call), aye, and a great
deal more besides, and be an honest man."  As
for changing his principles to suit the times, Mr.
Bye-Ends argues that it shows that the minister
" is of a self-sacrificing temper."

The argument for conformity is put so plausi-
bly that it is calculated to deceive the very elect;
and then as if by mere inadvertence we are
allowed a glimpse of the seamy side.  It is evi-

dent that the wits were not all banished from the
conventicles.

To those who are acquainted only with the
pale and interesting tea-drinking parsons of
nineteenth-century English fiction, there is something surprising in the clergymen one meets
in the pages of Fielding. They are all in such
rude health! There is not a suggestion of nervous prostration nor of minister's sore throat.
Not one of them seems to be in need of a vaca-
tion; perhaps because they are out of doors
all the time. Their professional duties were
doubtless done, but they are not obtruded on
the reader's attention.

The odious Chaplain Thwackum is chiefly remembered for his argument with the free-thinker
Square. Square having asserted that honor might
exist independently of religion, Thwackum re-
futes him in a manner most satisfactory. "When
I mention religion I mean the Christian religion,
and not only the Christian religion but the Protestant religion, and not only the Protestant religion but the religion of the Church of England;
and when I mention honor I mean that mode of

divine grace which is dependent on that religion."

" Thwackum," says the Gentle Reader, " was,
after all, an unworldly man.  He was content to
remain a mere hanger-on of the church when he
was capable of thoughts which were really in
great demand.  I have been looking over a huge
controversial volume by an author of that day,
and I found nothing but Thwackum argument
expanded and illustrated.  The author was made
a bishop for it."

As for Parson Trulliber, the Falstaff of divines, the less said about him the better.  The
curate Barnabas is a more pleasing character,
though hardly an example of spirituality.  He
reminds one of the good parson who, in his desire
for moderation, prayed that the Lord might lead
his people " in the safe middle path between right
and wrong."

When Joseph Andrews confessed his sins to
him, Barnabas was divided between his eagerness
to do his professional duty to the sinner, and the
desire to prepare the punch for the company
downstairs, a work in which he particularly
excelled.

" Barnabas asked him if he forgave his enemies
'as a Christian ought.'

" Joseph desired to know what that forgiveness
was.

"' That is,' answered Barnabas, ' to forgive
them — as — it is to forgive them as — in short,
to forgive them as a Christian.'

" Joseph replied ' He forgave them as much as
he could.'

"' Well ! Well ! ' said Barnabas, ' that will do ! '
He then demanded of him if he had any more
sins unrepented of, and if he had, to repent of
them as fast as he could ; . . . for some company
was waiting below in the parlor where the ingredients for punch were all in readiness, for that no
one could squeeze the oranges till he came."

Barnabas would have been shocked at the
demands of the Methodists for immediate repent-
ance, but on this occasion he was led into almost
equal urgency.

But Fielding more than atones for all the rest
by the creation of Parson Adams. Dear, delightful Parson Adams ! to know him is to love him !
In him the Church of England appears a little
out at the elbows, but in good heart. With the

appetite of a ploughman, and "a fist rather less
than the knuckle of an ox," he represents the
true church militant.  He has a pipe in his mouth,
and a short great coat which half conceals his
cassock, which he had "torn some ten years ago
in passing over a stile."  But however uncanon-
ical his attire, his heart is in the right place.

What a different world Parson Adams lived
in from that of George Eliot's Amos Barton,
bewildered with thoughts which he could not express.  "'Mr. Barton,' said his rural parishioner,
"'can preach as good a sermon as need be when
he writes it down, but when he tries to preach
without book he rambles about, and every now
and then flounders like a sheep as has cast itself
and can't get on its legs.'"

One cannot imagine Parson Adams floundering about, under any circumstances.  There is a
sturdy strength and directness about all he says
and does.  His simplicity is endearing but never
savors of weakness.

He sets great store by his manuscript sermons,
for which he seeks a publisher.  The curate Barnabas throws cold water on his plans.  The age,
he says, is so wicked that nobody reads sermons;

"'Would you think it, Mr. Adams, I intended to print a volume of sermons, myself, and they had the approbation of three bishops, but what do you think the bookseller offered me?'

"'Twelve guineas,' cried Adams.

"'Nay,' answered Barnabas, 'the dog refused me a concordance in exchange. . . . To be concise with you, three bishops said they were the best sermons that were ever writ; but indeed there are a pretty moderate number printed already, and they are not all sold yet.'"

The theology of Parson Adams was genially human. "'Can anything,' he said, 'be more derogatory to the honor of God than for men to imagine that the all-wise Being will hereafter say to the good and virtuous, Notwithstanding the purity of thy life, notwithstanding the constant rule of virtue and goodness in which thou walkedst upon earth; still, as thou didst not believe everything in the true orthodox manner, thy want of faith shall condemn thee? Or, on the other side, can any doctrine be more pernicious in society than the persuasion that it will be a good plea for a villain at the last day, — "Lord, it is true I never obeyed any of Thy commandments; yet punish me not, for I believe in them all?" ' "

This was not sound doctrine in the opinion of the itinerant bookseller. " 'I am afraid,' he said, ' that you will find a backwardness in the trade to engage in a book which the clergy would be certain to cry down.' "

The good parson had the clerical weakness for reading sermons in season and out of season. At a festive gathering there was a call for speeches, to which it was objected that no one was prepared for an address; " 'Unless,' turning to Adams, ' you have a sermon about you.'

" ' Sir,' said Adams, ' I never travel without one, for fear of what might happen.' "

Like other clergymen, he dabbled occasionally in politics. " 'On all proper seasons, such as at the approach of an election, I throw a suitable dash or two into my sermons, which I have the pleasure to hear is not disagreeable to Sir Thomas and the other honest gentlemen, my neighbors.' "

At one time he actively labored for the election of young Sir Thomas Booby, who had lately returned from his travels. He was elected, " 'and a fine Parliament man he was. They tell me he made speeches of an hour long, and I have been told very fine ones; but he could never persuade Parliament to be of his opinion.' "

Estimable, eloquent Sir Thomas Booby! How many orators have found the same result following their speeches of an hour long!

To the returned traveler who had engaged in a controversy with him, Parson Adams gave expression to his literary faith.

" ' Master of mine, perhaps I have traveled a great deal further than you, without the assistance of a ship. Do you imagine sailing by different cities or countries is traveling. I can go further in an afternoon than you in a twelvemonth. What, I suppose you have seen the pillars of Hercules and perhaps the walls of Carthage? . . . You have sailed among the Cyclades and passed the famous straits which took their name from the unfortunate Helle, so sweetly described by Apollonius Rhodius; you have passed the very spot where Dædalus fell into the sea; you have doubtless traversed the Euxine, and called at Colchis to see if there was another golden fleece.'

" ' Not I, truly,' said the gentleman. ' I never touched at any of these places.'

" ' But I have been in all these, ' replied Adams.

" ' Then you have been in the Indies, for there are no such places, I'll be sworn, either in the West Indies or in the Levant.'

" ' Pray, where is the Levant ? ' quoth Adams.

" ' Oho ! You 're a pretty traveler and not to know the Levant. You must not tip me for a traveler, it won't go here.'

" ' Since thou art so dull as to misunderstand me,' quoth Adams, ' I will inform thee. The traveling I mean is in books, the only kind of traveling by which any knowledge is acquired.' "

" There is a great deal to be said in defense of that opinion," says the Gentle Reader.

To turn from Parson Adams to the Vicar of Wakefield is to experience a change of spiritual climate. Parson Adams was a good man, and so was Dr. Primrose ; otherwise they were quite different. Was piety ever made more attractive to restless, over-driven people than in the person of the dear, non-resistant vicar. Here was a man

who might be reviled and persecuted, — but he
never could be hurried.

The Gentle Reader rejoices in the peace of the
opening chapters. "The year was spent in moral
and rural amusements. We had no revolutions
to fear, no fatigues to undergo, all our adventures were by the fireside, and all our migrations
were from the blue bed to the brown." And
good-natured Mrs. Primrose, absorbed in making
pickles and gooseberry wine, and with her ability
to read any English book without much spelling,
was an ideal minister's wife, before the days of
missionary societies and general information. It
was only her frivolous daughters who were
brought into society, where there was talk of
"pictures, taste, Shakespeare, and the musical
glasses." These subjects not then being supposed to have any esoteric, religious significance,
which it was the duty of the minister's wife to
discover and disseminate, she busied herself with
her domestic concerns without any haunting sense
that she was neglecting the weightier matters.
The vicar's favorite sermons were in praise of
matrimony, and he preached out of a happy
experience.

This peaceful scene bears the same relation to the trials that afterwards befell the good man that the prologue to the Book of Job does to the main part of it.   Satan has his will with Job, so also it happened with Dr. Primrose.   His banker absconds to Amsterdam, his daughter elopes with the wicked young squire who has the father thrown into prison, where he hears of the death of his wretched daughter who has been cast off by her betrayer.   Troubles came thick and fast ; yet did not the vicar hurry, nor for a moment change the even tenor of his way.   It was the middle of the eighteenth century, when piety was not treated as an elemental force.   It did not lift up its voice and cry out against injustice. The church was the patient Griselda married to the state, and the clergyman was a teacher of resignation.

Upon learning of his daughter's abduction, Dr. Primrose calls for his Bible and his staff, but he does not indulge in any haste unbecoming a clergyman.   He finds time in his leisurely pursuit to discourse most judiciously and at considerable length on the royal prerogative.   He remembers his duty to the landed gentry, and on his return from his unsuccessful quest remains several days to enjoy the squire's hospitality.

Was ever poetical justice done with more placidity and completeness than in the prison scene ? The vicar, feeling that he is about to die, proceeds to address his fellow wretches. He falls naturally into an old sermon on the evils of free-thinking philosophy, that being the line of the least resistance. The discourse being finished, it is without surprise and yet with real pleasure that we learn that he does not die; nor is his son, who was about to be hanged, hanged at all; on the contrary, he appears not long after handsomely dressed in regimentals, and makes a modest and distant bow to Miss Wilmot, the heiress. That young lady had just arrived and was to be married next day to the wicked young squire, but on learning that young gentleman's perfidy, " ' Oh goodness ! ' cried the lovely girl, ' how I have been deceived.' " The vicar's son being on the spot in his handsome regimentals, they are engaged in the presence of the company, and her affluent fortune is assured to this hitherto impecunious youth. And the daughter Olivia at the same time appears, it happening that she was not dead after all, and that she has papers to show that she is the lawful wife of the young squire. And the banker who ran away with the vicar's property has been captured and the money restored. In the mean time — for happy accidents never come singly — the wretch who was in the act of carrying off the younger daughter Sophy has been foiled by the opportune arrival of Mr. Burchell. And best of all, Mr. Burchell proves not to be Mr. Burchell at all, but the celebrated Sir William Thornhill, who is loyal to the constitution and a friend of the king. The Vicar is so far restored that he leaves the jail and partakes of a bountiful repast, at which the company is "as merry as affluence and innocence could make them."

Affluence as the providential, though sometimes long delayed, reward of innocence was a favorite thesis of eighteenth-century piety.

"It may sound very absurd," says the Gentle Reader, "to those who insist that all the happenings should be realistic; but the Vicar of Wakefield is a very real character, nevertheless; and he is the kind of a person for whom you would expect things to come out right in the end."

# Quixotism

~~∽◌◈◌∾~~

WHEN Falstaff boasted that he was not only witty himself but the cause of wit in other men, he thought of himself more highly than he ought to have thought. The very fact that he was witty prevented him from the highest efficiency in stimulating others in that direction. The atmospheric currents of merriment move irresistibly toward a vacuum. Create a character altogether destitute of humor and the most sluggish intelligence is stirred in the effort to fill the void.

When we seek one who is the cause of wit in other men we pass by the jovial Falstaff and come to the preternaturally serious Don Quixote. Here we have not the chance outcropping of "the lighter vein," but the mother lode which

the humorist finds inexhaustible. Don Quixote,
with a lofty gravity which never for an instant
relaxes, sets forth upon his mission. His is a
soul impenetrable to mirth ; but as he rides he
enlivens the whole country-side. Everywhere
merry eyes are watching him ; boisterous laughter
comes from the stables of village inns ; from castle windows high-born ladies smile upon him ; the
peasants in the fields stand gaping and holding
their sides ; the countenances of the priests relax,
and even the robbers salute the knight with mock
courtesy. The dullest La Manchan is refreshed,
and feels that he belongs to a choice coterie of
wits.

Cervantes tells us that he intended only a bur-
lesque on the books of chivalry which were in
vogue in his day. Had he done no more than he
intended, he would have amused his own generation and then have been forgotten. It would be
too much to ask that we should read the endless
tales about Amadis and Orlando, only that we
might appreciate his clever parody of them. A
satire lasts no longer than its object. It must
shoot folly as it flies. To keep on shooting at a
folly after it is dead is unsportsmanlike.

But though we have not read the old books of chivalry, we have all come in contact with Quixotism. I say we have all come in contact with it; but let no selfish, conventional persons be afraid lest they catch it. They are immune. They may do many foolish things, but they cannot possibly be quixotic. Quixotism is a malady possible only to generous minds.

Listen to Don Quixote as he makes his plea before the duke and duchess. "I have redressed grievances, righted the injured, chastised the insolent, vanquished giants. My intentions have all been directed toward virtuous ends and to do good to all mankind. Now judge, most excellent duke and duchess, whether a person who makes it his study to practice all this deserves to be called a fool."

Our first instinct is to answer confidently, "Of course not! Such a character as you describe is what we call a hero or a saint." But the person whose moral enthusiasm has been tempered with a knowledge of the queer combinations of goodness and folly of which human nature is capable is more wary, and answers, "That depends."

In the case of Don Quixote it depends very

much on the kind of world he lives in. If it should happen that in this world there are giants standing truculently at their castle doors, and forlorn maidens at every cross-roads waiting to be rescued, we will grant him the laurels that are due to the hero. But if La Mancha should not furnish these materials for his prowess, — then we must take a different view of the case.

The poor gentleman is mad, that is what tho curate and the barber say ; but when we listen to his conversation we are in doubt. If the curate could discourse half so eloquently he would have been a bishop long before this. The most that can be said is that he has some notions which are not in accordance with the facts, and that he acts accordingly ; but if that were a proof of madness there would not be enough sane persons in the world to make strait-jackets for the rest. His chief peculiarity is that he takes himself with a seriousness that is absolute. All of us have thoughts which would not bear the test of strict examination. There are vagrant fancies and random impulses which, fortunately for our reputations, come to nothing. We are just on the verge of doing something absurd when we recog-

nize the character of our proposed action ; and our
neighbors lose a pleasure.    We comfort ourselves
by the reflection that their loss is our gain.    Don
Quixote has no such inhibition ; he carries out
his own ideas to their logical conclusion.

The hero of Cervantes had muddled his wits
by the reading of romances.    Almost any kind
of printed matter may have the same effect if one
is not able to distinguish between what he has
read and what he has actually experienced.    One
may read treatises on political economy until he
mistakes the " economic man " who acts only according to the rules of enlightened self-interest
for a creature of flesh and blood.    One may read
so many articles on the Rights of Women that he
mistakes a hard-working American citizen who
spends his summer in a down-town office, in order
that his wife and daughter may go to Europe, for
that odious monster the Tyrant Man.    It is possible to read the Society columns of the daily
newspapers till the reader does not know good
society when he sees it.    An estimable teacher in
the public schools may devote herself so assidu-
ously to pedagogical literature that she mistakes
her schoolroom for a psychological laboratory,

with results that are sufficiently tragical. There
are excellent divines so learned in the history of
the early church that they believe that semi-pela-
gianism is still the paramount issue. There were
few men whose minds were, in general, better bal-
anced than Mr. Gladstone's, yet what a fine example of Quixotism was that suggested by Queen
Victoria's remark : " Mr. Gladstone always addresses me as if I were a public meeting." To
address a woman as if she were a public meeting
is the mistake of one who had devoted himself too
much to political speeches.

A thoroughly healthy mind can endure a good
deal of reading and a considerable amount of
speculation with impunity. It does not take the
ideas thus derived too seriously. It is continually making allowances, and every once in a while
there is a general clearance. It is like a gun
which expels the old cartridge as the new shot is
fired. When the delicate mechanism for the ex-
pulsion of exploded opinions gets out of order the
mind becomes the victim of " fixed ideas." The
best idea becomes dangerous when it gets stuck.
When the fixed ideas are of a noble and disinterested character we have a situation which ex-

cites at once the admiration of the moralist and the apprehension of the alienist. Perhaps this border-land between spiritual reality and intellectual hallucination belongs neither to the moralist nor to the alienist, but to the wise humorist. He laughs, but there is no bitterness or scorn in his laughter. It is mellow and human-hearted.

The world is full of people who have a faculty which enables them to believe whatever they wish. Thought is not, for them, a process which may go on indefinitely, a work in which they are collaborating with the universe. They do it all by themselves. It is the definite transaction of making up their minds. When the mind is made up it closes with a snap. After that, for an unwelcome idea to force an entrance would be a well-nigh impossible feat of intellectual burglary.

We sometimes speak of stubborn facts. Nonsense! A fact is a mere babe when compared with a stubborn theory. Let the theory, however extravagant in its origin, choose its own ground, and intrench itself in the mind of a well-meaning lady or gentleman of an argumentative turn, and I'll warrant you it can hold its own against a whole regiment of facts.

Did you ever attend a meeting of the society for the — perhaps I had better not mention the name of the society, lest I tread on your favorite Quixotism.  Suffice it to say that it has a noble purpose.  It aims at nothing less than the complete transformation of human society, by the use of means which, to say the least, seem quite inadequate.

After the minutes of the last meeting have been read, and the objects of the society have been once more stated with much detail, there is an opportunity for discussion from the floor.

" Perhaps there is some one who may give some new suggestions, or who may desire to ask a question."

You have observed what happens to the unfortunate questioner.  What a sorry exhibition he makes of himself !  No sooner does he open his mouth than every one recognizes his intellectual feebleness.   He seems unable to grasp the simplest ideas.   He stumbles at the first premise, and lies sprawling at the very threshold of the argument. " If what I have taken for granted be true," says the chairman, " do not all the fine things I have been telling you about follow necessarily ? "

"But," murmurs the questioner, "the things you take for granted are just what trouble me. They don't correspond to my experience."

"Poor, feeble-minded questioner!" cry the members of the society, "to think that he is not even able to take things for granted! And then to set up his experience against our constitution and by-laws!"

We sometimes speak of an inconsequent, harum-scarum person, who is always going off after new ideas, as quixotic. But true Quixotism is grave, self-contained, conservative. Within its own sphere it is accurate and circumstantial. There is no absurdity in its mental processes; all that is concealed in its assumptions. Granted the reality of the scheme of knight-errantry, and Don Quixote becomes a solid, dependable man who will conscientiously carry it out. There is no danger of his going off into vagaries. He has a mind that will keep the roadway.

He is a sound critic, intolerant of minor incongruities. When the puppet-player tells about the bells ringing in the mosques of the Moorish town, the knight is quick to correct him. "There you are out, boy; the Moors have no bells; they

only use kettledrums. Your ringing of bells in
Sansuena is a mere absurdity." Such absurdities were not amusing; they were offensive to
his serious taste.

The quixotic mind loves greatly the appearance
of strict logic. It is satisfied if one statement is
consistent with another statement; whether either
is consistent with the facts of the case is a curious matter which it does not care to investigate.
So much does it love Logic that it welcomes even
that black sheep of the logical family, the Fal-
lacy; and indeed the impudent fellow, with all
his irresponsible ways, does bear a family resemblance which is very deceiving. Above all is
there delight in that alluring mental exercise
known as the argument in a circle. It is an intellectual merry-go-round. A hobby-horse on
rockers is sport for tame intelligences, but a
hobby that can be made to go round is exciting.
You may see grave divines and astute metaphy-
sicians and even earnest sociologists rejoicing in
the swift sequence of their own ideas, as conclusion follows premise and premise conclusion, in
endless gyration. How the daring riders clutch
the bridles and exultingly watch the flying manes

of their steeds! They have the sense of getting somewhere, and at the same time the comfortable assurance that that somewhere is the very place from which they started.

"Didn't we tell you so!" they cry. "Here we are again. Our arguments must be true, for we can't get away from them."

Your ordinary investigator is a disappointing fellow. His opinions are always at the mercy of circumstances over which he has no control. He cuts his coat according to his cloth, and sometimes when his material runs short his intellectual garments are more scanty than decency allows. Sometimes after a weary journey into the Unknown he will return with scarcely an opinion to his back. Not so with the quixotist. His opinions not being dependent on evidence, he does not measure different degrees of probability. Half a reason is as good as a whole one, for the result in any case is perfect assurance. All things conspire, in most miraculous fashion, to confirm him in his views. That other men think differently he admits, he even welcomes their skepticism as a foil to his faith. His imperturbable tolerance is like that of some knight who, conscious of his

coat of mail, good-humoredly exposes himself to
the assaults of the rabble. It amuses them, and
does him no harm.

When Don Quixote had examined Mambrino's
enchanted helmet, his candor compelled him to
listen to Sancho's assertion that it was only a
barber's basin. He was not disposed to contro-
vert the evidence of the senses, but he had a sufficient explanation ready. "This enchanted helmet, by some strange accident, must have fallen
into the possession of one who, ignorant of its true
value as a helmet, and seeing it to be of the purest
gold, hath inconsiderately melted down the one
half for lucre's sake, and of the other half made
this, which, as thou sayest, doth indeed look like
a barber's basin; but to me, who know what it
really is, its transformation is of no importance,
for I will have it so repaired in the first town
where there is a smith that it shall not be sur-
passed or even equaled. In the mean time I will
wear it as I can, for something is better than
nothing, and it will be sufficient to defend me
from stones."

Where have you heard that line of argument,
so satisfying to one who has already made up his

mind? Yesterday, it runs, we had several excellent reasons for the opinion which we hold. Since
then, owing to investigations which we imprudently entered into before we knew where we
were coming out, all our reasons have been over-
thrown. This, however, makes not the slightest
difference. It rather strengthens our general
position, as it is no longer dependent on any particular evidence for its support.

We prate of the teaching of Experience. But
did you ever know Experience to teach anything
to a person whose ideas had set up an independent government of their own? The stern old
dame has been much overrated as an instructor.
Her pedagogical method is very primitive. Her
instruction is administered by a series of hard
whacks which the pupil is expected to interpret
for himself. That something is wrong is evident;
but what is it? It is only now and then that
some bright pupil says, " That means that I made
a mistake." As for persons of a quixotic disposition, the most adverse experience only confirms
their pre-conceptions. At most the wisdom
gained is prudential. After Don Quixote had
made his first unfortunate trial of his pasteboard

visor, "to secure it against like accidents in future he made it anew, and fenced it with thin plates of iron so skillfully that he had reason to be satisfied with his work, and so, without further experiment, resolved that it should pass for a good and sufficient helmet."

One is tempted to linger over that moment when Quixote ceased to experiment and began to dogmatize. What was the reason of his sudden dread of destructive criticism? Was he quite sincere? Did he really believe that his helmet was now cutlass proof?

For myself, I have no doubts of his knightly honor and of his transparent candor. He certainly believed that he believed; though under the circumstances he felt that it was better to take no further risks.

In his admirable discourse with Don Fernando on the comparative merits of arms and literature, he describes the effects of the invention of gunpowder.

" When I reflect on this I am almost tempted to say that in my heart I repent of having adopted the profession of knight-errantry in so detestable an age as we live in. For though no peril can

make me fear, still it gives me some uneasiness
to think that powder and lead may rob me of
the opportunity of making myself famous and
renowned throughout the world by the might of
my arm and the edge of my sword."

There is here a bit of uneasiness, such as comes
to any earnest person who perceives that the times
are out of joint. Still the doubt does not go very
deep. In an age of artillery knight-errantry is
doubtless more difficult, but it does not seem impossible.

It is the same feeling that must come now and
then to a gallant twentieth-century Jacobite who
meets with his fellow conspirators in an American city, to lament the untimely taking off of the
blessed martyr King Charles, and to plot for the
return of the House of Stuart. The circumstances under which they meet are not congenial.
The path of loyalty is not what it once was. A
number of things have happened since 1649; still
they may be treated as negligible quantities. It
is a fine thing to sing about the king coming to
his own again.

"But what if there is n't any king to speak
of?"

"Well, at any rate, the principle is the same."

I occasionally read a periodical devoted to the elevation of mankind by means of a combination of deep breathing and concentrated thought. The object is one in which I have long been interested. The means used are simple. The treatment consists in lying on one's back for fifteen minutes every morning with arms outstretched. Then one must begin to exhale self and inhale power. The directions are given with such exactness that no one with reasonably good lungs can go astray. The treatment is varied according to the need. One may in this way breathe in, not only health and love, but, what may seem to some more important, wealth.

The treatment for chronic impecuniosity is particularly interesting. The patient, as he lies on his back and breathes deeply, repeats, "I am Wealth." This sets the currents of financial success moving in his direction.

One might suppose that a theory of finance so different from that of the ordinary workaday world would be surrounded by an air of weirdness or strangeness. Not at all. Everything is most matter of fact. The Editor is evidently a sensible person when it comes to practical details, and, on occasion, gives admirable advice.

A correspondent writes: " I have tried your treatment for six months, and I am obliged to say that I am harder up than ever before. What do you advise? "

It is one of those obstinate cases which are met with now and then, and which test the real character of the practitioner. The matter is treated with admirable frankness, and yet with a wholesome optimism. The patient is reminded that six months is a short time, and one must not expect too quick results. A slow, sure progress is better, and the effects are more lasting. This is not the first case that has been slow in yielding to treatment. Still it may be better to make a slight change. The formula, " I am Wealth," may be too abstract, though it usually has worked well. A more concrete thought might possibly be more effective. Why not try, remembering, of course, to continue the same breathings, " I am Andrew Carnegie? "

Then the practitioner adds a bit of advice which was certainly worth the moderate fee charged:

"When the exercises are over, ask yourself what Andrew would do next.   Andrew would hustle."

A slight acquaintance with the pseudo sciences which are in vogue at the present day reveals a world to which only the genius of Cervantes could do justice.   We see Absurdity clothed, and in its right mind.   It is formally correct, punctiliously exact, completely serious, and withal high-minded. Until it comes in contact with the actual world we do not realize that it *is* absurd.

Religion and medicine have always furnished tempting fields for persons of the quixotic temper. Perhaps it is because their professed objects are so high, and perhaps also because their achievements fall so far below what we have been led to expect.   Neither spiritual nor mental health is so robust as to satisfy us with the usual efforts in their behalf.   Sin and sickness are continual challenges.   Some one ought to abolish them. An eager hearing is given to any one who claims to be able to do so.   The temptation is great for those who do not perceive the difference between words and things to answer the demands.

It is not necessary to go for examples either to fanatics or quacks.   Not to take too modern an

instance, there was Bishop Berkeley! He was a
true philosopher, an earnest Christian, and withal
a man of sense, and yet he was the author of
"Siris, a Chain of Philosophical Reflections and
Inquiries concerning the Virtues of Tar Water,
and divers other Subjects connected together, and
arising One from Another." It is one of those
works which are the cause of wit in other men.
It is so learned, so exhaustive, so pious, and the
author takes it with such utter seriousness!

Tar is the good bishop's Dulcinea. All his
powers are enlisted in the work of proclaiming
the matchless virtues of this mistress of his
imagination, who is "black but comely." Our
minds are prepared by a lyric outburst: —

> "Hail, vulgar Juice of never-fading Pine!
> Cheap as thou art! thy virtues are divine,
> To show them and explain (such is thy store),
> There needs much modern and much ancient Lore."

For this great work the author is well equipped.
Plato, Aristotle, Pliny, and the rest of the an-
cients appear as vanquished knights compelled to
do honor to my Lady Tar.

Other specifics are allowed to have their virtues, but they grow pale before this paragon.

Common soap has its admirers; they are treated magnanimously, but compelled to surrender at last. "Soap is allowed to be cleansing, attenuating, opening, resolving, sweetening; it is pectoral, vulnerary, diuretic, and hath other good qualities; which are also found in tar water. . . . Tar water therefore is a soap, and as such hath all the medicinal qualities of soaps." To those who put their faith in vinegar a like argument is made. It is shown that tar water is not only a superior kind of soap, but also a sublimated sort of vinegar; in fact, it appears to be all things to all men.

To those who incline to the philosophy of the ancient fire-worshipers a special argument is made. "I had a long Time entertained an Opinion agreeable to the Sentiments of many ancient Philosophers, that Fire may be regarded as the Animal Spirit of this visible World. And it seemed to me that the attracting and secreting of this Fire in the various Pores, Tubes, and Ducts of Vegetables, did impart their specifick Virtues to each kind, that this same Light, or Fire, was the immediate Cause of Sense and Motion, and consequently of Life and Health to animals; that on Account of this Solar Light or Fire, Phœbus was in the ancient Mythology reputed the God of Medicine. Which Light as it is leisurely introduced, and fixed in the viscid juice of old Firs and Pines, so setting it free in Part, that is, the changing its viscid for a volatile Vehicle, which may mix with Water, and convey it throughout the Habit copiously and inoffensively, would be of infinite Use in Physic." It appears therefore that tar water is not only a kind of soap, but also a kind of fire.

Yet is not Quixote himself more careful to avoid all appearance of extravagance? The author shrinks from imposing conclusions on another. After an elaborate argument which moves irresistibly to one conclusion, he stops short. " This regards the Possibility of a Panacea in general; as for Tar Water in particular, I do not say it is a Panacea, I only suspect it to be so." Yet he must be a churlish reader who could go with him so far and then refuse to take the next step. Nor can a right-minded person be indifferent to the moral argument in favor of "Tar Water, Temperance, and Early Hours." If tar water is to be known by the company it keeps, it is to be commended.

There is a great advantage in taking our example from another age than ours. Our enjoyment of the bishop's Quixotism does not cast discredit on any similar hobby of our own day. "However," as the author of Siris remarked, "it is hoped they will not condemn one Man's Tar Water for another Man's Pill or Drop, any more than they would hang one Man for another's having stole a Horse."

Indeed, of all quixotic notions the most extreme is that of those who think that Quixotism can be overcome by any direct attack. It is a state of mind which must be accepted as we accept any other curious fact. As well tilt against a cloud as attempt to overcome it by argument. It is a part of the myth-making faculty of the human mind. A myth is a quixotic notion which takes possession of multitudes rather than of a single person. Everybody accepts it; nobody knows why. You can nail a lie, but you cannot nail a myth, — there is nothing to nail it to. It is of no use to deny it, for that only gives it a greater vogue.

I have great sympathy for all mythical characters. It is possible that Hercules may have

been an amiable Greek gentleman of sedentary
habits. Some one may have started the story
of his labors as a joke. In the next town it
was taken seriously, and the tale set forth on its
travels. After it once had been generally accepted, what could Hercules do? What good
would it have been for him to say, "There's not
a word of truth in what everybody is saying about
me. I am as averse to a hard day's work as any
gentleman of my social standing in the community. They are turning me into a sun-myth, and
mixing up my private affairs with the signs of
the zodiac! I won't stand it!"

Bless me! he would have to stand it! His
words would but add fuel to the flame of admiration. What a hero he is; so strong and so
modest! He has already forgotten those feats
of strength! It is ever so with greatness. To
Hercules it was all mere child's play. All the
more need that we keep the stories alive in order
to hand them down to our children. Perhaps we
had better touch them up a bit so that they may
be more interesting to the little dears. And so
would begin a new cycle of myths.

After Socrates had once gained the reputation

for superlative wisdom, do you think it did any
good for him to go about proclaiming that he
knew nothing? He was suspected of having
some ulterior design. Nobody would believe him
except Xanthippe.

When after hearing strange noises in the night
Don Quixote sallies forth only to discover that
the sounds come from fulling hammers instead of
from giants, he rebukes the ill-timed merriment
of his squire. "Come hither, merry sir! Suppose these mill hammers had really been some
perilous adventure, have I not given proof of the
courage requisite to undertake and achieve it?
Am I, being a knight, to distinguish between
sounds, and to know which are and which are not
those of a fulling mill, more especially as I have
never seen any fulling mills in my life?"

If the mill hammers could only be transformed
into giants, how easy the path of reform! for it
would satisfy the primitive instinct to go out and
kill something. I have heard a temperance ora-
tor denounce the Demon Drink so roundly that
every one in the audience was ready to destroy
the monster on sight. The solution of the liquor

problem, however, was quite a different matter. The young patriot who conceives of the money power under the terrifying image of an octopus resolves at once to give it battle. When elected to the legislature he meets many smooth-spoken gentlemen whose schemes are so plausible that he readily assents to them, — but not an octopus does he see. Yet I believe that were he to see an octopus he would slay it.

Perhaps there is no better test of a person's nature than his attitude toward Quixotism. The man of coarse, unfriendly humor sees in it nothing but a broad farce. He greets the misadventures of Don Quixote with a loud guffaw. What a fool he was not to know the difference between an ordinary inn and a castle!

There are persons of a sensitive and refined disposition to whom it is all a tragedy, exquisitely painful to contemplate. Alas, poor gentleman, with all his lofty ideals, to be so buffeted by a world unworthy of him!

But this refinement of sentiment comes perilously near to sentimentalism. Cervantes had the more wholesome attitude. He appreciated the

valor of Don Quixote. It was genuine, though
the knight, owing to circumstances beyond his
own control, had been compelled to make his
visor out of pasteboard. He had heroism of soul;
but what of it! There was plenty more where it
came from. A man who had fought at Lepanto,
and endured years of Algerine captivity, was not
inclined to treat manly virtue as if it were a rare
and delicate fabric that must be preserved in a
glass case. It was amply able to take care of
itself. He knew that he couldn't laugh genuine
chivalry away, even if he tried. It could stand
not only hard knocks from its foes, but any
amount of raillery from its friends.

The bewildered soldier who mistakes a harm-
less camp follower for the enemy must expect
to endure the gibes of his comrades; yet no one
doubts that he would have acquitted himself nobly
if the enemy had appeared. The rough humor
of the camp is a part of its wholesome discipline.

Quixotism is a combination of goodness and
folly. To enjoy it one must be able to appreciate
them both at the same time. It is a pleasure
possible only to one who is capable of having
mixed feelings.

When we consider the faculty which many good people have of believing things that are not so, and ignoring the plainest facts and laws of nature, we are sometimes alarmed over the future of society. If any of the Quixotisms which are now in vogue should get themselves established, what then?

Fortunately there is small need of anxiety. When the landsman first ventures on the waves he observes with alarm the keeling over of the boat under the breeze, for he expects the tendency to be followed to its logical conclusion. Fortunately for the equilibrium of society, tendencies which are viewed with alarm are seldom carried to their logical conclusion. They are met by other tendencies before the danger point is reached, and the balance is restored.

The factor which is overlooked by those who fear the ascendency of any quixotic notion is the existence of the average man. This individual is not a striking personality, but he holds the balance of power. Before any extravagant idea can establish itself it must convert the average man. He is very susceptible, and takes a suggestion so readily that it seems to prophesy the complete overthrow of the existing order of things. But was ever a conversion absolute? The best theologians say no. A great deal of the old Adam is always left over. When the average man takes up with a quixotic notion, only so much of it is practically wrought out as he is able to comprehend. The old Adam of common sense continually asserts itself. The natural corrective of Quixotism is Sancho-Panzaism. The solemn knight, with his head full of visionary plans, is followed by a squire who is as faithful as his nature will permit. Sancho has no theories, and makes no demands on the world. He leaves that sort of thing to his master. He has the fatalism which belongs to ignorant good nature, and the tolerance which is found in easy-going persons who have neither ideals nor nerves. He has no illusions, though he has all the credulity of ignorance.

He belongs to the established order of things, and can conceive no other. When knight-errantry is proposed to him, he reduces that also to the established order. He takes it up as an honest livelihood, and rides forth in search of forlorn maidens with the same contented jog with which

he formerly went to the village mill. When it
is explained that faithful squires become gover-
nors of islands he approves of the idea, and begins to cherish a reasonable ambition. Knight-
errantry is brought within the sphere of practical
politics. Sancho has no stomach for adventures.
When his master warns him against attacking
knights, until such time as he has himself reached
their estate, he answers : —

"Never fear, I 'll be sure to obey your worship
in that, I 'll warrant you ; for I ever loved peace
and quietness, and never cared to thrust myself
into frays and quarrels."

When Sancho becomes governor of his snug,
land-locked island, there is not a trace of Quixotism in his executive policy. The laws of Chivalry have no recognition in his administration ;
and everything is carried on with most admirable
common sense.

It is an experience which is quite familiar to
the readers of history. "All who knew Sancho,"
moralizes the author, "wondered to hear him talk
so sensibly, and began to think that offices and
places of trust inspire some men with understanding, as they stupefy and confound others."

Mother wit has a great way of evading the con-
sequences of theoretical absurdities. Natural law
takes care of itself, and preserves the balance.
So long as Don Quixote can get no other follower
than Sancho Panza, we need not be alarmed.
There is no call for a society for the Preservation
of Windmills.

After all, there is an ambiguity about Quixotism. They laugh best who laugh last; and we
are not sure that satire has the last word. Was
Don Quixote as completely mistaken as he
seemed? He mistook La Mancha for a land of
romance, and wandered through it as if it were
an enchanted country.

The Commentator explains to us that in this
lay the jest, for no part of Spain was so vulgarly
commonplace. Its villages were destitute of
charm, and its landscape of beauty. La Mancha
was a name for all that was unromantic.

" I cannot make it appear so," says the Gentle
Reader, who has come under the spell of Cervantes. "Don Quixote seems to be wandering
through the most romantic country in the world.
I can see

'The long, straight line of the highway,
    The distant town that seems so near,
  .    .    .    .    .    .    .    .

White crosses in the mountain pass,
    Mules gay with tassels, the loud din
Of muleteers, the tethered ass
That crops the dusty wayside grass,
And cavaliers with spurs of brass
    Alighting at the inn ;

White hamlets hidden in fields of wheat,
  .    .    .    .    .    .    .    .
White sunshine flooding square and street,
Dark mountain-ranges, at whose feet
The river-beds are dry with heat, —
    All was a dream to me.'

" Through this enchanted country it is pleasant to wander about in irresponsible fashion,
climbing mountains, loitering in secluded valleys,
where shepherds and shepherdesses still make
love in Arcadian fashion, meeting with monks,
merchants, muleteers, and fine gentlemen, and
coming in the evening to some castle where one
is lulled to sleep by the splash of fountains and
the tinkle of guitars; and if it should turn out
that the castle is only an inn, — why, to lodge
in an inn of La Mancha would be a romantic
experience ! "

The Spain of the sixteenth century is to us as truly a land of romance as any over which a knight-errant roamed. It seems just suited for heroic adventure.

Some day our quixotic characters may appear to the future reader thus magically conformed to the world they live in, or rather, the world may be transformed by their ideals.

"They do seem strange to us," the Gentle Reader of that day will say, " but then we must remember that they lived in the romantic dawn of the twentieth century."

# Intimate Knowledge and Delight

❦

IN the affairs of the mind we are all " Indian
givers." We will part with our most cherished
convictions for a merely nominal consideration,
such as " for the sake of the argument," — even
when we do not really care for arguments. But
let no one be deceived into thinking that this is
the end. Renunciation usually has some mental
reservation, or at least some saving ambiguity.

You may see a saint, in his enthusiasm for
disinterested virtue, give up all claim to personal
happiness. But does he expect to be taken at his
word and to live miserably ever after? Not he!
Already, if he be a true saint, he has begun to
enjoy the beatific vision.

I know a teacher of religion who is inclined to rebel against what seems to him to be the undue emphasis upon faith. For himself, it seems a wholesome thing to do a little doubting now and then, and he looks upon this as a religious exercise. He affirms that the characteristic attitudes of the spiritual man can be expressed in terms of skepticism as well as of belief. It is all one whether the matter be put positively or negatively. Materialism he treats as a form of dogmatism based on the appearance of things. The religious mind is incredulous of this explanation of the universe and subjects it to a destructive criticism. The soul of man is full of " obstinate questionings of sense and outward things." Yet this same person, when he forgets his argument, is apt to talk like the rest of us. After all, it is some kind of faith that he is after, even when he pursues it by the methods of skepticism. In his most radical moods he never lets his convictions slip away from him ; at least, they never go so far away that he cannot get them again.

In like manner I must confess that I am an Indian giver. In giving over to Science all claim to the domain of Knowledge, and reserving to my

friend the Gentle Reader only the right of way
over the picturesque but less fruitful fields of
Ignorance, I was actuated by the purest motives.
At the time it seemed very magnanimous, and,
moreover, it saved the trouble of a doubtful contest.

But now that so much has been given away, I
am visited by compunctions, and, if it is not too
late, I will take back part of the too generous
gift.   Let us make a distinction, and instead of
treating knowledge as if it were indivisible, let
us speak, after the manner of Swedenborg, of
knowledges.   The greater number of knowledges
we will make over without question to Science
and Philosophy; the knowledges which are concerned with laws and forces and with the multi-
tudinous facts which are capable of classification.
But for the Gentle Reader and his kind let us
reserve the claim to a knowledge of some things
which cannot be classified.   I hardly believe that
they will be missed; they are not likely to be
included in any scientific inventory; their value
is chiefly in personal association.

There is a knowledge of persons as well as of
things, and in particular there is a knowledge

of certain persons to whom one is drawn in close friendship. Emerson, in his essay on Milton, speaks of those who come to the poet with "intimate knowledge and delight." It is, after all, convenient to treat this feeling of delightful intimacy as a kind of knowledge. If it is not that, what is it?

The peculiarity of this kind of knowledge is that it is impossible to formulate it; and that the very attempt to do so is an offence. The unpardonable sin against friendship is to merge the person in a class. Think of an individual as an adult Caucasian, " an inhabitant of North America, belonging to the better classes," as to religion a moderate churchman, in politics a Republican, and you may accumulate a number of details interesting enough in a stranger. You may in this way " know where to place him." But if you do actually place him there, and treat him accordingly, he has ceased to be your friend.

A friend is unique. He belongs to no categories. He is not a case, nor the illustration of a thesis. Your interest is neither pathological nor anthropological nor statistical. You are concerned not with what he is like, but with what

he is.   There is an element of jealous exclusive-
ness in such knowledge.

In the Song of Songs, after the ecstatic praise
of the beloved, the question is asked : —

> "What is thy beloved more than any other beloved, that thou
>     dost so adjure us ? "

The answer is a description of his personal
perfections : —

> "My beloved is white and ruddy,
>
> .   .   .   .   .   .   .   .   .   .
>
> His locks are bushy, and black as a raven.
> His eyes are like doves beside the water brooks.
>
> .   .   .   .   .   .   .   .   .   .
>
> His aspect is like Lebanon, excellent as the cedars,
> His mouth is most sweet: yea, he is altogether lovely.
> This is my beloved, and this is my friend,
> O daughters of Jerusalem."

Do you think that the daughters of Jerusalem
would be so tactless as to reply that they had
seen a number of handsome youths with bushy
black hair and languishing eyes and fine forms,
and that they represented an admirable type of
manly beauty?  That would be to confess that
they had not seen the beloved, for he was unlike
all others.   "My beloved is marked out with a
banner among ten thousand."

The knowledge that is required is not contained in a catalogue of the points in which he resembles the nine thousand nine hundred and ninety-nine; it is a recognition of the incommunicable grace that is his own.

Even in ordinary social intercourse the most delicate compliment is to treat the person with whom you are talking as an exception to all rules. That he is a clergyman or a commercial traveler tells you nothing of his inner life. That is left for him to reveal, if it so pleases him. Even a king grows tired of being addressed in terms appropriate to royalty. It is a relief to travel incognito, and he is flattered when he is assured that no one suspects his station in life. It makes him feel that he is not like the ordinary run of kings.

No one likes to be pigeon-holed or reduced to a formula. We resent being classed as old or middle-aged or young. Why should we be confounded with our coevals? We may not be any better than they are; but we are different. Nor is it pleasant to have our opinions treated as if they were the necessary product of social forces. There is something offensive in the curiosity of

those who are all the time asking how we came
by our ideas. What if they do bear a general
resemblance to those of the honest people who
belong to our party and who read the same
newspaper. We do not care to be reminded of
these chance coincidences. Because one has found
it convenient and economical to buy a ready-made
suit of clothing, it does not follow that he is willing to wear the tag which contains the statement
of the price and size. These labels were very
useful so long as the garment was kept in stock
by the dealer, but the information that they convey
is now irrelevant.

This sensitiveness in regard to personal identity
is strangely lacking in many modern students of
literature. They treat the man of genius as a
phenomenon, to be explained by other phenomena
and used to illustrate a general law. They love
to deal in averages and aggregates. They describe minutely the period to which a writer belongs, its currents of thought, its intellectual
limitations, and its generally received notions.
With a knowledge of antecedent conditions there
is the expectancy of a certain type of man as the
result. Our minds are prepared for some one

who resembles the composite photograph which is first presented to us. We are, for example, given an elaborate account of the Puritan movement in England. We form a conception of what the Puritan was, and then we are introduced to Milton. Our preconceptions stand in the way of personal sympathy.

The method of the Gentle Reader is more direct. He is fortunate enough to have read Milton before he has read much about him, and he returns to the reading with ever fresh delight. He does not think of him as belonging to a past age. He is a perpetual contemporary. The seventeenth century gave color to his words, but it did not limit his genius.

Seventeenth century Independency might be, as a general thing, lacking in grace, but when we turn away from Praise-God-Barebones to John Milton we find it transformed into a —

> " divine philosophy,
> Not harsh and crabbed as dull fools suppose,
> But musical as is Apollo's lute,
> And a perpetual feast of nectared sweets."

Into its austere beauty, into its wide free spaces, into its sensuous charms, no one but Milton can

conduct us. We must follow not as those who
know beforehand what is to be seen or heard, but
as those who are welcomed by a generous householder who brings out of his treasures things new
and old.

We come upon a sublime spirit —

> " Pure as the naked heavens, majestic, free."

That is Milton ; but it is Milton also who can
sing of —

> " Jest and youthful Jollity,
> Quips and Cranks and wanton Wiles,
> Nods and Becks and wreathed Smiles
> Such as hang on Hebe's cheek,
> And love to live in dimple sleek,
> Sport that wrinkled Care derides,
> And Laughter holding both his sides."

If this be Puritanism, it is Puritanism with a
difference. Did any one in a few words give
such a picture of mirth —

> " So buxom, blithe, and debonair ? "

Was this the real Milton? Why not? His
radiant youth was as real as his blindness and
his old age. And Milton the political pamphlet-
eer was real too, though his language was not
always that which might have been expected

from the author of " Paradise Lost." We pass
lightly over pages of vituperation which any one
might have written, and then come upon splen-
did passages which could have come from him
alone. The sentiment of democratic equality is
invested with a dignity which makes all the pretensions of privileged orders seem vulgar. Here
is the Milton who is invoked to —

> " Give us manners, virtue, freedom, power ! "

In these moments we become aware of a man who
was not to be explained by any general rule.

To one who takes delight in the personality
of Milton, even " Paradise Lost " is not a piece of
unmitigated sublimity. It is full of self-revela-
tions. The reader who has come to share Milton's passion for personal liberty and scorn for
a " fugitive and cloistered virtue " is curious to
know how he will treat his new theme. In the
" Areopagitica " he had frankly treated the " Fall
of Man " as a " fall upward." " Good and evil
we know in the field of this world grow up together almost inseparably ; and the knowledge
of good is so involved and interwoven with the
knowledge of evil, and in so many cunning re-
semblances hardly to be discerned, that those

confused seeds which were imposed on Psyche
as an increased labor to cull out and sort asun-
der, were not more intermixt.  And perhaps
that is the doom which Adam fell into of knowing good and evil; that is to say, of knowing
good by evil.  As therefore the state of man
now is, what wisdom can there be to choose,
what continence to forbear without the knowledge of evil. . . . That virtue, therefore, which
is but a youngling in the contemplation of evil,
and knows not the utmost that vice promises to
her followers, and rejects it, is but a blank virtue,
not a pure. . . . Since, therefore, the knowledge
and survey of vice is in this world so necessary
to the constituting of human virtue, and the
scanning of error to the confirmation of truth,
how can we more safely and with less danger
scout into the region of sin and falsity than by
reading all manner of tractates and hearing all
manner of reasons."

What would such an adventurous spirit make

> " Of man's first Disobedience and the Fruit
> Of that Forbidden Tree, whose mortal taste
> Brought Death into the World and all our woe,
> With loss of Eden " ?

What would Milton make of Adam in his sheltered Paradise? And what would one whose whole life had been a passionate protest against the idea of submission to mere arbitrary power do with the element of arbitrariness which the theology of his day attributed to the Divine Ruler? And what of Satan?

> "One who brings
> A mind not to be changed by Place or Time.
> The mind is its own place, and in itself
> Can make a Heaven of Hell, a Hell of Heaven.
> What matter where, if I be still the same?"

There is a note in that proud creed that could not be altogether uncongenial to one who in his blindness could —

> "still bear up and steer
> Right onward. What supports me, dost thou ask?
> The Conscience, Friend, t' have lost them overplied
> In liberty's defense, my noble task;
> Of which all Europe rings from side to side.
> This thought might lead me through this World's vain mask
> Content though blind, had I no better Guide."

In its ostensible plot "Paradise Lost" is a tragedy; but did Milton really feel it to be so? One fancies — though he may be mistaken — that as Adam and Eve leave Paradise he hears a sigh of relief from the poet, who was himself ever a lover of "the Mountain Nymph, sweet Liberty." At any rate, there is an undertone of cheer.

> "Some natural tears they dropped, but wiped them soon,
>  The World was all before them where to choose
>  Their place of rest, and Providence their guide."

Adam, when the old sheltered life is over, and the possibilities of the new life of struggle were revealed, —

> "Replete with joy and wonder thus replied.
>  O goodness infinite, goodness immense!
>  That all this good of evil shall produce,
>  And evil turn to good; more wonderful
>  Than that which by creation first brought forth
>  Light out of darkness! full of doubt I stand,
>  Whether I should repent me now of sin
>  By me done and occasioned or rejoice
>  Much more that much more good thereof shall spring."

That Adam should treat the loss of Eden in such a casual manner, and that he should express a doubt as to whether the estate into which his fall plunged the race was not better than one in which no moral struggle was necessary, was not characteristic of seventeenth-century theology, — but it was just like Milton.

There is no knowledge so intimate as that possessed by the reader of one book. It is an esoteric joy. The wisdom of the ages concentrated into one personality and then graciously communicated to the disciple has a flavor of which the multitudes of mere scholars know nothing. To them Wisdom is a public character.

> " Doth not Wisdom cry,
>     And understanding put forth her voice ?
>   In the top of high places
>     Where the paths meet she standeth."

But the disciple is not content with such publicity. He shuns the crowded highways, and delights to hear wisdom speaking in confidential tones.

In a little settlement in the far West I once met a somewhat depressed-looking man who remained silent till a chance remark brought a glow of enthusiasm to his eyes.

" Oh," he cried, " you have been reading the Ruins."

My remark had been of a kind that needed no special reading to account for it. It merely expressed one of those obvious truths which are likely to occur to the majority of persons. But

to him it seemed so reasonable that it could only
come from the one source of wise thought with
which he was acquainted.

" The Ruins " proved to be a translation of
Volney's " Ruins of Empire." I fear that I
must have given the impression of greater familiarity with that work than was warranted by the
facts, for my new-found friend received me as a
member of the true brotherhood. His tongue
was unloosed, and his intellectual passions, so
long pent up, were freed. Had we not both
read " The Ruins " ! It was to him more than a
book; it was a symbol of the unutterable things
of the mind. It was a passionate protest against
the narrow opinions of his neighbors. It stood
for all that was lifted above the petty gossip of
the little community, and for all that united him
to an intellectual world of which he dreamed.

As we talked I marveled at the amount of
sound philosophy this lonely reader had ex-
tracted from " The Ruins." Or had it been that
he had brought the wisdom from his own medita-
tion and deposited it at this shrine? One can
never be sure whether a text has suggested the
thought or the thought has illuminated the text.

When it happens that the man of one book has chosen a work of intrinsic value, the result is a kind of knowledge which is of inestimable worth. It is deeply interfused with the whole imaginative life, it is involved in every personal experience.

The supreme example of such intimate knowledge was that which generations of English speaking men had of the Bible. Apart from any religious theory, this familiarity was a wonderful fact in the history of culture. It meant that the ordinary man was not simply in his youth but throughout his life brought into direct contact with great poetry, sublime philosophy, vivid history. These were not reserved for state occasions ; they were the daily food of the mind. Into the plain fabric of western thought was woven a thread of Oriental sentiment. Children were as familiar with the names and incidents of remote ages and lands as with their own neighborhood.

The important things about this culture of the common people was that it came through mere reading. The Bible was printed " without note or comment." The lack of critical apparatus and of preliminary training was the cause of many incidental mistakes; but it prevented the greatest mistake of all, — that of obscuring the text by the commentary.

In these days there has been a great advance in critical scholarship. Much more is known about the Bible, at least by those who have made it the object of special study; but there is a suspicion that fewer persons know the Bible than in the days when there were no " study classes," but only the habit of daily reading.

The Protestant insistence upon publishing the Scriptures without note or comment was an effort to do away with the middle-men who stood between the Book and its readers. Private judgment, it was declared, was a sufficient interpreter even of the profoundest utterances. This is a doctrine that needs to be revived and extended till it takes in all great literature.

To come to a book as to a friend, to allow it to speak for itself, without the intrusion of a third person, this is the substance of the whole matter. There must be no hard and fast rules, no preconceived opinions. Because the author has a reputation as a humorist, let him not be received with

an expectant smile.  Nothing can be more disconcerting to his sensitive spirit; and besides,
how can you know that he has not a very serious
message to communicate?  Because he is said to
be capable of sublimity, do not await him with
overstrained sensibilities.  Perhaps you may find
him much less sublime and much more entertaining than you had anticipated.  If the sublime
vision does come, you will appreciate it all the
more if it comes upon you unawares.

" As cloud on cloud, as snow on snow, as the
bird on the air, and the planet on space in its
flight, so do nations of men and their institutions
rest on thoughts."

If this be so, can there be any knowledge more
important than the knowledge of what a man
actually thinks.  " A penny for your thoughts,"
we say lightly, knowing well that this hidden
treasure cannot be bought.  The world may be
described in formal fashion as if it were an un-
changing reality; but how the world appears to
each inhabitant of it he alone can declare.  Or
perhaps he cannot declare it, for most of us find
it impossible to tell what we really think or feel.
In attempting to do it we fall into conventional-

ity, and succeed only in telling what we think other people would like to have us think. Only now and then is one born with the gift of true self-expression. In his speech we recognize a real person, and not the confused murmur of a multitude. Institutions and traditions do not account for him; this thought is the more fundamental fact. Here is a unique bit of knowledge. There is no other way of getting at it than that of the Gentle Reader, — to shut out the rest of the world and listen to the man himself.

**The Riverside Press**

*Electrotyped and printed by H. O. Houghton & Co.*
*Cambridge, Mass., U. S. A.*